DEATH SCENES

A HOMICIDE DETECTIVE'S SCRAPBOOK

TEXT BY KATHERINE DUNN

EDITED AND DESIGNED BY SEAN TEJARATCHI

Death Scenes
© 1996 Feral House
ISBN 0-922915-29-6

A catalogue of publications is available upon request from the above address or visit: www.feralhouse.com

15 14 13 12

Feral House publications are distributed to the book trade by Publishers Group West

Thanks from the editor to all those who contributed to the creation of this book. To Scott Gregory and Tom Robinson of the Photo Research Group in Portland, Oregon for their assistance, advice and opinions. Thanks also to Scott Gregory for the scrapbook photographs on pages 166 and 167. To Christy Aguirre for typesetting finesse and eleventh hour assistance. To Greg Maffei at Grey Matter Design in Portland for invaluable technical assistance. And my thanks to Toni Lee Smith for technical assistance and for her support. And my gratitude to Adam for the opportunity.

CONTENTS:

THE PURPOSE OF THIS COLLECTION OF HOMICIDE
PICTURES IS TO SHOW THE WORK OF THE PEACE OFFICER AND
HIS PROBLEMS.

IT WILL GIVE YOU AN IDEA OF WHAT THEY HAVE TO
CONTEND WITH WHILE PERFORMING THEIR DUTIES IN PROTECT-
ING LIVES AND PROPERTY.

AFTER VIEWING THIS WORK IT WILL UNDOUBTEDLY
BRING ABOUT A BETTER UNDERSTANDING BETWEEN THE LAW
ENFORCEMENT OFFICER AND THE PUBLIC WHICH HE SERVES.

IT IS ALSO INCUMBENT UPON YOU, AS A CITIZEN
AND TAXPAYER, IN THE COMMUNITY IN WHICH YOU RESIDE,
TO EXTEND TO YOUR LAW ENFORCEMENT AGENCY YOUR FULLEST
COOPERATION IN ASSISTING IN ITS SOLVING THE PROBLEMS
THAT COME BEFORE IT.

AS YOU WILL SEE, MOST OF THESE CRIMES ARE
SOLVED AND THE GUILTY PROSECUTED WHICH PROVES THAT
CRIME DOES NOT PAY.

PLEASE HANDLE THIS BOOK WITH RESPECT.

Jack Huddleston

"WHAT THEY HAD TO CONTEND WITH..."
INTRODUCTION BY KATHERINE DUNN

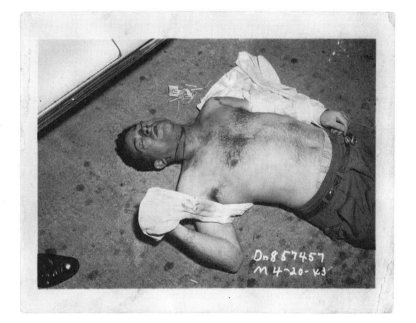

The body has lain for a few hours in the Van Nuys alley, long enough for the midday sun to encourage the evolving course of putrefaction. Waves of blowflies feed, lay eggs, drape the whole head in shifts like a dark handkerchief that puffs and falls over the face as if from a sleeper's breath. Their buzzing is the sporadic snore of the exhausted. The medical examiner crouches beside the corpse and the flies do not disperse but lift and settle again. Undisturbed for one full day the corpse would twitch with hatching maggots. The still air is heavy with the metallic tang of blood and the first sweet taint of gut decay. The reek of the emptied bowel is sharpened by the ammoniac bite of spilt urine or sour vomit.

Violent death makes visible that which was never meant to be seen—the glistening innards, the secret apparatus beneath the skin. These unfamiliar sights are not easily comprehended. Workers new to the job, rookie cops and ambulance drivers, struggle with the mess. Their eyes reel at ripped distortions that blur a formerly human identity.

Experienced death workers throw a professional switch in their brains and see the face more clearly. Their eyes methodically link dismembered limbs, realign a rictus grin, and separate identity from wreckage. Cooly. As connoisseurs. For the investigators a dead body is not so much victim as evidence, the ultimate clue to the workings of the perpetrator.

Banked anger smolders in the official grammar introducing Jack Huddleston's scrapbook of horrors. He created this monument to death, depravity and human foible during a Los Angeles area police career that spanned the decades from 1921 to the early 50s. The records of his working life are apparently buried in the mounds of antique files stored in municipal basements and warehouses. Our inquiries to the LAPD produced a blunt refusal from the head of the Personnel Division. The staff was far too busy to bother with archaeological excavations for mere historical purposes. All we know of Jack Huddleston is the internal evidence of his scrapbook, which suggests, among other things, that he spent years as a detective on the homicide detail for LAPD, and that he blamed us, the oblivious citizenry, for the contents of his collection.

What the do-gooders label "de-sensitization" has a value as well as a price. Some of us can't afford to be shocked by catastrophe. The surgeon, the burn ward nurse, emergency room attendants, paramedics, firefighters and cops, all those who scrape the still-screaming remains out of car wrecks, must cultivate their off-switch. Those who can't learn to crack wise and discuss baseball over a corpse

must find a gentler line of work. The rumor is that city cops get strange from what they see,

JACK HUDDLESTON

their eyes flattening or sinking into sockets as deep and hollow as rat holes.

Maybe Huddleston was one of those, his view of the world permanently skewed. Maybe certain images, specific faces, electrified his dreams, and rasped his waking thoughts. Some cases, especially the unsolved, may have gnawed

at him for years. Maybe his only friends were cops who knew the same bad jokes. Maybe his lone brooding in the dark made his wife and children uneasy. The odds are he didn't like to be touched.

The original scrapbook is large, six inches thick. Its stiff cardboard covers have disappeared over time and what is left are hundreds of black and white photos glued onto 18 X 24 inch sheets of heavy paper that is now mummy-brown with age and crumbling at the edges.

The deaths represented here are nearly all "unnatural"—accidents, suicides, murders, and legal executions. The majority of the photos are of actual homicide scenes, corpses lying where they were found, snapped by police photographers for use by investigators and as documentation in court. Many are morgue shots taken during the autopsy. The date and the photographers name are often scratched directly onto the negative. This is not artful imagery, but a stark, pragmatic recording of evidence. The intended audience for these pictures was limited—cops, medical examiners, prosecutors, a jury.

The scrapbook's creator has provided notes and captions for many of the exhibits. Some are typed on separate pieces of paper and then glued in. Many are inked or penciled directly onto the page in his own hand. Huddleston's comments are usually couched in dry cop-talk, salted with occasional flippant remarks. In several instances he has returned to the photo to add a notation of the arrest and sentencing, or execution of the perpetrator.

Over the years Jack Huddleston must have pulled these pictures from many sources. He probably found some of them by scrounging around the photo lab, scooping them out of waste baskets or closed case files. Photographers and other detectives, knowing his interest, might have given him their more spectacular examples. Maybe he paid for some of them. Almost

certainly, some of them were from cases he worked himself. And Southern California was the ideal place for his obscure collecting hobby.

JACK HUDDLESTON (LEFT) WITH THE ROBBERY AND HOMICIDE DEPARTMENT LOS ANGELES, 1938

The word from the crime statisticians of the U.S. Justice Department is that the Southern and Western regions of the United States have a higher rate of violent crime than does the crowded North East. This contradiction of our

Noir stereotypes is hard to fathom here in the open spaces where there are so few high-rise slums, where the cities sprawl wide rather than deep. Nobody knows why for sure, but there are theories. There's more turf west of the Mississippi than East of it. More people. More towns and cities. Some scholars claim that when enough people congeal in a given area the crime rate assumes "city" status and stays there. Then too, there's the weather. For months of every year the North is frozen and treacherous. Every venture past your own doorway has a fatal potential. In those parts the general crime rate drops dramatically in winter and soars in summer. The proposed explanation is that burglars and bashers, robbers and rapists don't like the cold any more than the rest of us. On the Pacific coast, where winters are mild, the crime rate doesn't vary as much from season to season. In the South, and in the dense warrens of Southern California, it's always summer for crime.

But not all of the crimes in the scrapbook occurred in Los Angeles. There are news shots as well as police photos from famous cases such as the Lindbergh kidnapping, the Valentines Day Massacre, the FBI shooting of John Dillinger, and other events far from Los Angeles. Huddleston probably had access to these original prints through his cop cronies around the country.

Still, most of the deaths recorded here were in Huddleston's locale, and were uncelebrated even by the news of the day. These are the understandable suicides of the hopeless, the dreary, pathetic crimes of domestic passion, revenge or drunken rage. They are the by-products of massive mental derangement or of stupid panic during haphazard robberies. Some, more notable at the time, seemed important to Huddleston—the famed "Black Dahlia" mystery, the bizarre hermaphrodite "Blue Beard" series. The "unsolved" crimes, such as the "Lipstick Murder," apparently

JACK HUDDLESTON (LEFT) AT
"FOOTPRINT ASSOCIATION"
EVENT CA. 1938

nagged at the collector, and are recorded with an almost tangible irritation.

But Huddleston's interests were expansive and exploratory. Other images, variations on his focused theme, trickle through his scrapbook. There are reminders of the punishment that waits for the perp—prisons and executioners' tools from the ax to the electric chair. There are

photos of Jack and his police pals at official events and in goofy ceremonies of a social club called "The Footprint Association." Some of his exhibits fall into the category of sideshow entertainments which were enormously popular throughout Huddleston's career.

The result is an historical and cultural artifact, a time capsule that reveals seldom seen sub-stratas of American life and death. One of the scrapbook's immediate effects is to deflate rosy nostalgia with the proof that there were no "good old days."

It is startling to realize that these crimes were committed in a time we tend to consider innocent—before television, before the special effects violence of modern movies, most of them even before the mass horrors of WW II. Our capacity for savagery and eccentricity hasn't changed in the last fifty years. Any of the crimes represented here could pop out of tomorrow's headlines.

The evidence that the crimes of Jack

Huddleston's era were as brutal and deranged as anything that happens today offers a grim lesson in the nature of the human animal. And it warns against the quick-fix hysteria that blames the forms or content of entertainment mediums and demands censorship as a solution.

The scrapbook is also evidence of Jack Huddleston's personal obsessions. It is an assemblage of found objects collected in no discernible pattern. Huddleston seems to have pasted in the pictures as they came to him. Though many of the photos and cases are dated, they are not in chronological order. A corpse discovered in 1932 may appear on the same page with others found and photographed years later.

It could be argued that the very randomness of the scrapbook's design reflects the unpredictability and disconnectedness of a detective's work, never knowing what may confront him next, what he'll have to cope with.

We can imagine him coming home from work with a manila envelope, tossing it on a

HUDDLESTON,
IN CENTER

dresser or desk. He would wait until after supper to open the envelope, to arrange and label his latest find. Did he share this hobby with his wife? Did he frighten his children with these images and the stories that went with them? Or was it his private pornography, locked away until he was alone in the house for a few hours?

The most recent photos in the scrapbook are from 1951 and 1952. It seems reasonable to surmise that Huddleston must have retired around that time. Sometime in the next three decades, Jack Huddleston apparently died. His scrapbook surfaced in the mid-1980s when the owners of a used book store in Burbank bought it as part of a larger lot of books from an estate sale. The estate was evidently that of Jack Huddleston's widow.

It's hard to imagine Mrs. Huddleston putting this scrapbook out on the grand piano with the framed family pictures, or leafing through it as a cherished souvenir of her late husband. More likely it was boxed in a closet after his death, an enduring embarrassment like a dead minister's porn stash or an old soldier's necklace of dried ears or collection of Nazi paraphernalia.

When the bookstore proprietors saw the scrapbook they knew it would interest one of their employees, the underground artist Nick Bougas. They gave it to him.

A self-described "gore hound," Bougas was fascinated. He kept the scrapbook on his coffee table at home where it made an energetic conversation piece for his guests. But he soon noticed that the pages were beginning to crumble and tear as they were handled. The scrapbook would not last forever. Bougas decided to preserve as much as he could of the strange artifact. Using selected stills from the scrapbook, Bougas created the remarkable videotape film, "Death Scenes" which is narrated by Anton LaVey, the High Priest of the Church of Satan, who was himself a police photographer for the San Francisco Police Department in the 1950s.

During his work with the scrapbook, Bougas actually searched for and visited many of the Los Angeles locations noted in the captions. A surprising number of the houses, hotels and other buildings noted here still exist, their bloody histories invisible to the modern inhabitants.

Bougas stood, for example, in the very parking lot on the exact spot where, some forty years before in February of 1946, "MISS MAY (CHUCKIE) DASPARRO AGE 32 A PROSTITUTE" was found with her clothes ripped

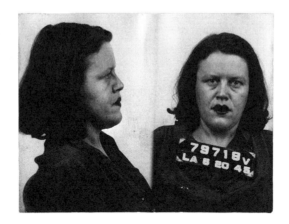

off, a handkerchief stuffed into her mouth, and twenty-two stab wounds in her left breast. The crime scene photos of Dasparro's body are stark, flash-lit pools surrounded by night. The bright photos taken during the autopsy

show the swarm of weeping, eye-shaped wounds in her breast. Her relaxed dead face is barely recognizable as the same wary living woman in the mug shots taken during one of her prostitution arrests. The hand-written note appended to the typed caption of this series informs us that Chuckie got her justice if only after the fact. Two months after her death her murderer was arrested, tried and sentenced to five years to life in San Quentin.

In 1921, young Jack Huddleston had his picture taken wearing the uniform and badge of the Santa Monica Police Department. This was apparently his first police job. It was common for a cop to start on the force of a smaller town and then move up to the wider opportunities of the big city departments. Huddleston became a cop at a time when most Americans were born at home and died the same way, surrounded by kin. It was common for families to arrange final portraits of their dead. Professional photographers were paid to lug their bulky equipment into home parlours and funeral chapels to shoot elderly men in luxurious coffins, beautifully dressed infants held up to the lens by mothers frozen in shock, young women with ornate hair-styles lounging on sofas as though napping. These memorial photos were displayed on mantles and shared with grieving friends and relatives.

Thirty years later, at the end of Huddleston's career, formal portraits of the dead were no longer fashionable. The very idea was labeled morbid and ghoulish in the determinedly cheerful post-war, post-Depression boom times. Miraculous antibiotics had just been introduced, vaccines protected the young from the diseases that had decimated earlier child populations. Birth and death had been shuttled behind hospital screens to be dealt with by white-gowned professionals. For the first time in human history people could afford the luxury of declaring death to be in bad taste.

But people went on dying and the practice of making memorial photos didn't end, it simply submerged and became private. Reports from photo-processors and printers indicate that many families use their own Instamatic to create

last images of lost loved ones. But these mementos, like those of earlier eras, are simulations of peaceful sleep. They are always taken after the mortician has prettied up the corpse. Nobody wants a snapshot of young Frankie the way he looked when they dragged him out from under the train. Those terrible pictures were then and are now sequestered, taboo. Except to Jack Huddleston and his colleagues.

Throughout Huddleston's life popular culture flaunted an unabashed fascination with oddities, marvels and horrors. Freaks were the staple of circus side-shows. "Ripley's Believe It Or Not" was the most widely syndicated feature in American newspapers. The ink drawings and short captions assigned the same wonderment to everything from a carrot with the profile of Abe Lincoln, to the Hindu snake charmer and the one-legged girl who won the dance marathon. The clever Ripley collected his choicest items in best-selling books, and inspired droves of imitators.

It's not surprising that Jack Huddleston reveals a dead-pan humor in the various oddities included in his scrapbook. The effect is sometimes comic relief, sometimes a ferocious irony. The overall impact is a classical thread of comedy woven through tragedy, the inextricable tangling of the absurd and the agonizing. Modern sensibilities may be shocked and bewildered by Huddleston's cavalier treatment of painful topics. He was intrigued, for instance, by dramatic medical maladies.

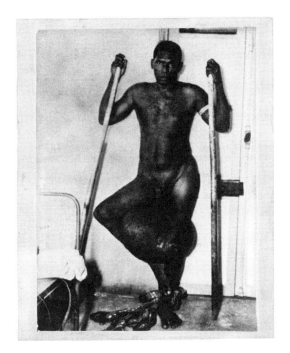

A clear and rather sympathetic nude portrait of a man with Elephantiasis of the scrotum triggers the predictable questions and their inevitable answers in the mind of the viewer—how does the poor devil walk? Slowly. How can he sit down? Carefully. Why doesn't he have the damned thing nipped off so he can lead a normal life? Surely that tortured bag no longer produces viable sperm.

But then you remember the modern and amiable business tycoon whose three-piece suit hides an ornate collar-to-ankle tattoo. His private portions are pierced and knobbed in chrome. He takes an occasional holiday to explore the outer regions of his own sensibility by slowly injecting his scrotum with larger and larger volumes of sterile saline solution, gradually stretching it to just such extremes as this. He stays calmly in his hotel room, doing business by phone, ordering room service and enjoying the sensation for the several days it takes for his body to absorb the excess fluid and for his scrotal sac to resume its usual deeply wrinkled size. He claims now to have stretched the sac so successfully that he can inject a full three liters of fluid into his scrotum.

So who knows? Maybe the man in the scrapbook also finds an exquisite and secret pleasure in his involuntary pachydermic burden.

Huddleston blithely labels one enormous corpse as another victim of elephantiasis, and his caption goes on to define the affliction at some length. This is bothersome because the heap of dead flesh lolling on this extra large morgue table does not look like a case of elephantiasis at all, but a monstrous case of morbid and moribund obesity. The poor corpse is uniformly grotesque, pendulous, a sumo wrestler whose belly and heart have fallen prey to gravity.

Is our Jack deliberately pulling our leg? Or is he fooled too? We must remember that Huddleston's formality is the institutional delivery of cop talk, not education. His spelling

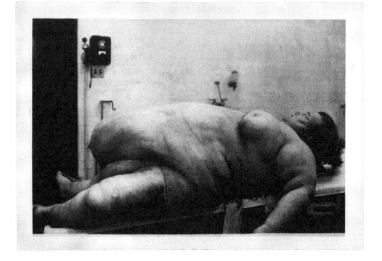

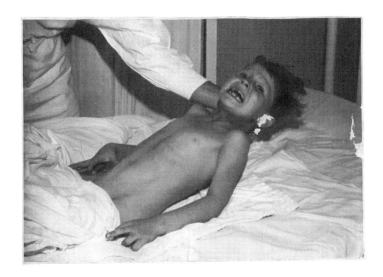

is serviceable but wobbly, his grammar is official rather than literate. His data is more street than academy. And how could a rake-lean Californian who came to manhood between the great wars have an exact knowledge of tropical parasites? No, Jack is merely struck and hypothesizing. One thing he knew was strangeness when he saw it.

The illness theme is further demonstrated by large tumors, skin afflictions worthy of a Roger Corman monster, victims of tetanus, or as Huddleston calls it "Lock-Jaw," and the ravaged evidence of leprosy (which, we suspect, may actually be tertiary syphilis). There are

several tense portraits labeled "hydrophobia." The faces strain with so much pain and panic that we yearn for a Kevorkian mercy, remembering that when these photos were taken there was probably little choice but to strap the victims down and let them scream themselves to death. The child, especially. Could her parents sit beside her through hours of agony and not do something with a pillow or smuggled baseball bat to end it?

Some of the deaths depicted here were accidental. One remarkable shot shows several young people, festively dressed couples, toppled by creeping, irresistible sleep in the midst of a party. A faulty heater spewing carbon monoxide in a poorly ventilated room has killed them all.

The most arresting of the accident images is the car wreck victim whose neatly severed head sits in the middle of a dirt road. The young man's head, eyes closed, is so calm and balanced

that he might be relaxing at the beach, buried to his chin in sand. In the spirit of those souvenir mystics who see Elvis' face in a spaghetti stain, or portraits of the Virgin Mary in the craw of the Dungeness Crab, Huddleston has inked the companion photo of the headless body with an arrow pointing to a gleaming reflection in the neck stump. His hand-printed caption reads, "Showing image of HEAD in the NECK."

Our Jack has a lightsome touch, at times, and an eye for the mysteries of the ages. There is no indication, for example, that the two shrunken heads from Borneo played a role in any crime

He gives us fetching transvestite and hermaphrodite prostitutes apparently for their amazement value. The blonde cross-dresser is Hollywood glamorous, if a trifle disarrayed in custody. The beefy Captain of detectives leans over her, fascinated. The photograph is a joke for Huddleston, perhaps because the Captain looks so smitten that we can imagine this moment as the prelude to a grappling, a stolen kiss at the cell door, a fumbling at the skirted crotch and an explosion of hetero-cop rage when his hand clutches the concealed evidence.

In another living portrait a dainty hermaphrodite may have been crying, or just snatched in from the rain. Her mascara is beginning to run, and she looks side-long, pitifully flirtatious into the camera. But in the accompanying close-up of a hermaphrodite crotch, all dignity and personality are obliterated by clinical rubber gloves hoisting, fingering and pointing at the mysteries of dual equipment. This photo is so similar in angle and lighting to the morgue shots of the dead that we wonder if these are before and after versions of the same now-defunct creature, or an indignity inflicted on a living victim, or even a morgue shot of some entirely different person.

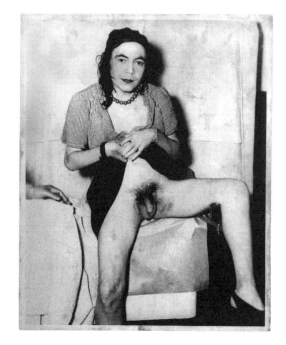

except their own creation in a far-off place where it may have been socially acceptable. But the photos have fallen into Jack's hands and he can't resist them.

And there are sideshow jokes—"Frenchie," the lewd, nude, tattooed man proudly displays the clunky kama sutra inked from his neck to his ankles. There is a special charm in two views of a meek but versatile exhibitionist with his pants cut away like chaps in front and back. The caption explains he wore a long overcoat and would flash his penis at women and his ass at men.

Sardonic juxtapositions are one of Huddleston's delicate pleasures. On one page, for example, a clever kitten is perched, peeing, on a chamber pot next to a shot of the nude suicide corpse of Jean Harlowe's husband. His thin body has fallen awkwardly into his own blood pool, still clutching a pistol. His soft, pale flesh is feminine, muscle-less. Only the hair on his legs marks him as male and adult. Huddleston has drawn a question mark beneath the caption, but we can't be sure whether he doubts that this death was self-inflicted, or is wondering if he's mis-labeled the corpse.

On the same page, above the comic novelty of the kitten, the sad, sagging cellulite of Mrs. Irene McCarthy is exposed in three views. She is discovered naked and battered, wearing only gleaming new black high-heeled shoes. What seems to be a towel is tied tightly over her face. A broad leather belt is buckled snugly around her neck.

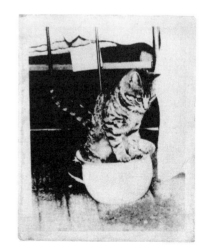

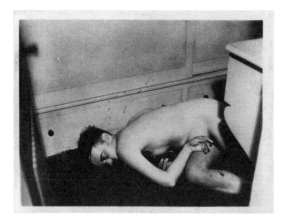

Her belly is ripped open but bloodless, as though some savage post mortem cesarean had been performed. A chipper "Uncle Sam" style tattoo is visible on her right thigh.

Huddleston offers us no context or motive for this horrendous attack. He simply notes with satisfaction that her murderer was gassed to death at San Quentin nine months later. The justice of the execution is explained tersely in quotation marks, "He Killed three women."

XXXXXXX

In his captions, Jack Huddleston often designates the race of the victim or the perpetrator using language typical for his era. "Negro," he will write, or "Jap," surrounding the terms with quotation marks which he uses intermittently throughout the scrapbook for emphasis. He doesn't, however, display hostility or contempt for any race. He doesn't have obvious fun at the expense of any race—although vaudeville, minstrel shows and radio programming were doing precisely that during his career. His clinical presentation of Asians, Pacific islanders, whites, Hispanics and Blacks provides a glimpse of the melting pot that Los Angeles was in the process of becoming. It should also remind us that the law enforcement agencies of the region functioned mainly as the rich white people's police, keeping the poor and those of other races at bay in designated ghettos. Real estate boosters sold Los Angeles as a crime-free glamour zone of orange groves and Hollywood glitter, while the cops were triggering and brutally suppressing the Hispanic "Zoot Suit Riots."

Huddleston's world was the distopian L.A. of Raymond Chandler, where worms squirm beneath the glossy veneer.

Most often Huddleston's captions are crisply professional. They provide a spartan notation with dates, the location, the method of dispatch, if it isn't obvious in the photo, and the names of the victim and the perpetrator. If the killer is unknown, the crime unsolved, the lack is noted by a question mark. "Killed by husband with iron bar," he says. Or "Killed by Mother," or "Killed by ? shotgun."

These are not depictions from the normal course of human events. Each of these photographs is proof that something happened. Something went wrong. Each photo is the climax of a drama, a mystery that begs to be deciphered. We are hobbled Sherlocks combing second-hand images for clues, interpreting insufficient data with the tools of raw fancy that recognizes ourselves as both victim and perpetrator. The imaginary process becomes part of the fascination—as if a glass window were installed in your abdomen and you stand naked at a mirror watching the peristaltic python of your own gut moving in slow, convulsive rhythms beyond your conscious volition. Jack puts us in this position because his commentary fails us so frequently.

In some cases the photos are left to tell the story without any help from the collector. There is no caption, for example, to explain the diner booth where two men were half-way through their plates of spaghetti when somebody dished out the bullets that spoiled their appetites. We can surmise they were bad guys killed by other bad guys. We can connect the stereotypes and think Italian mobsters because of the spaghetti. We understand that this was a quick, efficient, and probably professional hit, because the two corpses slump at the table almost tidily, with no evidence of turmoil.

Sometimes Jack gives us a bare bones version of the actual story—as in his caption for the photos of 27 year-old Mrs. Georgiana S., a blonde shown sprawled on the flowered carpet at the foot of her flowered drapes in mid-December of 1945. The photographs reveal details of her life. In keeping with the Christmas season, two ornamental snow globes share a nearby coffee table with a glass candy dish and an ash tray. The disruptions in this tidy room—a fallen lamp, the blood stains on the carpet—are the by-products of murder intruding on a proud housekeeper, an

attractive woman. Her eyebrows are immaculately plucked in thin arcs, her nails are painted. Her fanciful shoes have cuban heels and a fluff of feathers at the arch. We are left wondering why her skirt is rucked up to her waist. Was it an accident in the way she fell? Or did her murderer pull it up to look? Her legs are smooth and bare and loose garters show at the edge of her under pants. Had she just come home and taken off her stockings (which were fragile, expensive, and hard to find in those times) to preserve them and relax? Her prettiness elaborates the brief account of her death that Huddleston provides. "Killed by her discharged overseas husband, Julius F. S. age 29. He came home and found her living with Joseph O. age 28. He killed them, then he committed suicide."

The gun is not visible. We suppose it was a military issue. The mens' bodies do not appear in this end of the room though they may be dead just outside the frame. The only hint of male presence is a sports jacket hanging crookedly from the back of a chair. It is a civilian cut, not the uniform of one who came home from World War II just in time for Christmas.

In one of his brief tales, Huddleston's language goes far beyond his usual stark jargon. The headline is typically brutal, "Murder Rape and Robbery." The crime took place in September of 1942. The night photograph is

harshly lit by flash. Mrs. Lillian Stratton, age 74, lies on the lawn of her home in the dark. An emergency medical worker crouches to press an oxygen mask over her face. "Mr. Stratton age 81 years with tear dimmed eyes is on the right with a neighbor," Huddleston tells us. "The shock defeated his will to live. He joined his wife in death with a broken heart (1-15-43)." This is one of only two instances in the scrapbook where Huddleston reveals his sympathies. The recording of the old man's date of death suggests that this was a case our Jack investigated himself, and followed up. He has left a space in the typed line for the name of the perpetrator, but only a question mark remains there. The crime was never solved.

Suicide seems to draw out Huddleston's jocular wit. A full page of people hanging in closets, garages and barns is wryly labeled "A Little Throat Trouble." Contempt is a common reaction to those who destroy themselves. Suicide is the rift in the species, the leaking crack in our own fiber, and it scares us more than murder. Yet in this whole ferocious chronicle, Jack Huddleston allows himself only two soft moments, only two expressions of genuine sympathy. One of those is for the old man mentioned above, whose wife was murdered. The other is for a suicide. A young boy is sprawled against a work bench in some rough shed with the fatal revolver beside him. His handsome face bears some resemblance to the youthful portrait of Huddleston himself in his 1921 patrolman's uniform. The cop's block printing remarks,

> SUICIDE 15 YRS OLD
> CAUSED BY
> A BROKEN HOME, AND
> A BROKEN HEART

If we were certain before that Huddleston was cold to the core, we must reconsider when he repeats this crucial, hackneyed phrase, "a broken heart." After all he's seen and probably done, Jack H. believes men can die of a broken heart. And he, who does not like to be touched, is touched by that.

XXXXXX

We say these things lightly—"I shoulda stood in bed," meaning we should have avoided trouble. We say "safe in our beds at night" or "he died at home in his bed," meaning peacefully, quietly, without pain, as opposed to "with his boots on." The bed is a nest, the sheltered den where we feel safest and most at ease. We relax there. We make our private and personal love. We allow ourselves that most complete vulnerability—Sleep. But Detective Jack shows us the bed as another kind of place entirely—an arena of terror. This is the place where love goes wrong and tears you to pieces. This is the place where the predator flings down his prey and rips it for pleasure. Where the stranger creeps to find you. Where your own mother pounces on your innocent sleep and punishes you for everything that ever happened to her. Where your drunken father rapes and strangles you. This is the suffocating cage where

the last agony of the suicide plays itself out, where an acid drip eats at the mind until lead sucked from a steel tube is the only conceivable anaesthetic.

These are the lumpy, butt-sprung fold-out sofas, the headless Hollywood work benches of

the hookers, barred cribs meant to protect the very infants who die in them, desperate, moldy mats on grimy floors, and the Murphy beds that lift or roll into a dark cavity in the wall of a cheap apartment, maybe with somebody still inside.

These are the frail wire beds of rented rooms, their mattresses stained and thin. The screech of metal springs is the voice of love or murder. In this world beds have legs to keep you out of reach of rats and roaches—the vermin parasites of human filth. You can smell the heavy staleness of sleep in the rumpled sheets, the blood stiffened pillows.

Some of the scrapbook's most piercing images are not the corpses themselves but the mundane objects that surround them, the familiar every-day items that tell a tale of the lives that led to this death. By these signs we know that most of the victims depicted here were poor. The thin linoleum floor coverings come in cheezy geometric or fake flowered patterns from the Depression and before. Carpets are cheap and worn. The mass-produced wooden chairs with their chipped paint and familiar shapes are replicas of the thousands that any one of us has seen in junk shops, bought at yard sales, sat on for breakfast in our mother's kitchen or our own. Common wallpaper patterns, towel racks, the tiles of a bathroom floor, the still popular design of a saucepan or a salt shaker lend a frightening credibility to scenes of carnage. We struggle to deny the evidence of violence, to thrust it into the realm of fantasy, but these homely effects are things we understand and recognize despite ourselves. Their presence near the battered dead taints them with irony and omen, and the artifacts lend their own reality to the unimaginable.

A group of four photos depicts the messy room in which a young man and woman apparently lived and died. The tight arrangement of the matching spool bed, dresser and chest of drawers around an ancient gas heater tells us how small and crowded this room was. There is no caption but the evidence of the photos suggest that the man fired a shotgun into the woman's face and then served himself the same way. Clothes are strewn on the floor. His sport coat is draped with other garments over

the foot of the bed. Both their faces have been obliterated but they were obviously attractive, stylish and young.

What's left of his head has neatly trimmed hair. The flesh of his neck is smooth and firm.

His pleated trousers show signs of a recent pressing. A detachable bow tie lies on the dressing table among her cosmetics. In death he has collapsed with one arm around a serious shoe-shine box. Was it a personal grooming tool? Or did he

use it to earn money? His left shoe is muddy at the heel, but thin soled, gleaming and quite elegant as it rests near the shotgun that killed them both. The shotgun lies across the opening of a small closet, where the long striped skirt of her evening dress drapes across a worn and battered pair of his oxfords.

A tangle of clothes hangers on the closet floor may be the usual disorder or a sign of hasty packing before the cataclysm struck. Was she leaving him? Is that the significance of the strewn clothing on which she has fallen?

She may have been dressing or packing when her end arrived. A fabric belt is still caught in her upraised hand. She is wearing a bracelet and a watch, and on her left ankle, above the Cuban heeled pumps, a delicate chain. Her limbs are soft and slim.

These photos were taken in January of 1947 and no object in the room would be out of place in a cheap hotel fifty years later as I write this. One thing in particular tweaks the eye—the rug that softens the wood floor. The dead woman and her spewed clothing have fallen on it. The blood from her former face has run across it to a dark pool on the floor. Identical rugs are still available in every cheap import store on the West coast. It can be found in nearly every college dormitory, and in half the first apartments of working girls across the nation. It is a pale, matted cotton rug from Mexico, elaborately and colorfully embroidered with the flowering branches of the tree of life.

But the off-switch doesn't seem to work for the toddler who was raped and strangled. No sarcastic bright side comes to mind. Even Huddleston cannot conjure irony in these dark zones. He is, in fact, rendered speechless, leaving the most hideous of these photos caption-less, unexplained. The effect is so painful that we come away convinced that he wanted us to see this—to punish us as he was punished by seeing it.

The angriest photos, the most brutal, are the dead children. The toughest cops, so the stories go, get bizarre when the victim is a child. In most of us instinct and emotion rebel at the very idea. Most of these infants were killed by their mothers, of course. Who else would have a motive? And after you've seen a few of these scenes a caustic bright side inevitably occurs to you—if your mother is that crazy she'd do a lousy job of raising you. This child's life would have been hell. Death is easier. Less painful. And if she kills her offspring she eliminates her own defective line from the gene pool.

This wooden resignation seems natural, a temporary civilian off-switch, a mental protection from violations of a species-deep passion to protect.

Newspapers and broadcasters make daily decisions about what is permissible to show to "a family audience." Over the decades, clothing has shrunk and views of healthy living flesh expanded. Critical body parts are still proscribed in America's mainstream venues, but high on the unofficial "banned" list are dead bodies. As one photo editor explained to us, "If you absolutely have to show a dead body, you wait until it's

decently covered by a sheet or zipped into a body bag. You definitely don't show the face. No dead faces."

Or at least, no dead American faces. Recent news coverage of the war in vivisected former Yugoslavia goes for the audience throat with an occasional obvious corpse. Those dying of starvation in Somalia and other disaster areas were fair game for heart-wrenching depictions. Magazines and some television coverage ran astounding (though usually long-distance) shots of heaped corpses or bloated bodies clogging waterways during the bloody fury in the African nation of Rwanda.

There are, perhaps, dueling imperatives at work in the depiction of these foreign corpses. The reporters themselves are outraged by the atrocities, and deliberately provoke a response from the public in an effort to goad a govern-

mental response. This is not sensationalism, they might claim, this is gore for a good cause.

But it's hard not to recall the esteemed National Geographic magazine and the joys it offered those who were adolescents during Jack Huddleston's police career. At a time when only downright brown-bag pornography provided unobstructed images of female

nipples in the U.S.A., the respectable old "Geographic" delivered glaringly bared boobs conveniently attached to colorful tribeswomen in far off places where shirts were considered unnecessary.

Relaxed and lushly tinted tits were presented as evidence of the extremes encountered by the Geographic's intrepid explorers, and an emblem of difference between the civilized, literate, clothed and largely pale-faced subscribers and these exotically ignorant savages. It's tempting to conclude that race was the cut-off line. At least we can't recall any Geographic features on the sauna practices of the civil Swedes. The apparent rationale was that black, brown or golden women were too alien to be subjects for sexual consideration by the caucasian readers, so showing their breasts was no more challenging to con-

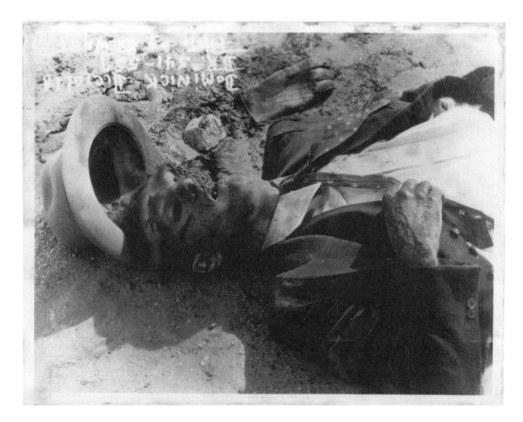

vention than color snaps of the buffalo cow's teats or the micturating lioness.

In much the same way we are shown corpses from afar because a cozy American audience will not be offended by identifying too closely with the victims and whatever long-distance sympathy can be mustered will help to right the wronged and rescue the innocent.

These are lies, of course. Just as the blushing young once poured for hours over grandpa's stack of Geographics, the news watchers and readers of today are drawn in guilty, clucking fascination to mounds of massacred remains, to rows of earthquake victims sprawled side by side on dirt roads for counting and identification.

Nudity and explicit sex are far more easily available now than are clear images of death. The quasi-violence of movies and television dwells on the lively acts of killing—flying kicks, roaring weapons, crashing cars, flaming explosions. These are the mortal equivalents of old-time cinematic sex. The fictional spurting of gun muzzles offer flirtation and seduction but stop a titillating instant short of actual copulation. The results of such aggressive vivacity remain a mystery. The corpse itself, riddled and gaping, swelling or dismembered, the action of heat and bacteria, of mummification or decay are the most illicit pornography.

The images we seldom see are the aftermath of violent deaths. Your family newspaper will not print photos of the puddled suicide who jumped from the fourteenth floor, no car wrecks with the body parts unevenly distributed, no murder victim sprawled in his own juices. Despite the endless preaching against violent crime, despite the enormous and avid audience for tales of mayhem, these images are taboo.

The prohibition is not a new one. Even the 19th century crime scene photos of Mary Kelly, the last victim in the Jack the Ripper case, are still suppressed. Few beyond the walls of Scotland Yard have ever seen the full mania of what he did to her. The image of her lying in the bed—her severed breasts flopped like frying eggs on the table nearby, her face flayed away except for the two eyes still staring out—is considered too much for the public to bear.

This is the reality as opposed to the fantasy image of violence provided by cinematic fictions in which the victim dies fast if not instantly from one stab wound, one shot in the heart. That happens, of course. But anyone who's worked in an emergency room knows you also might be stabbed 20 times and still walk into the E.R. carrying your intestines in both hands and asking earnest questions, "How am I doing?" or "Does my insurance cover this?"

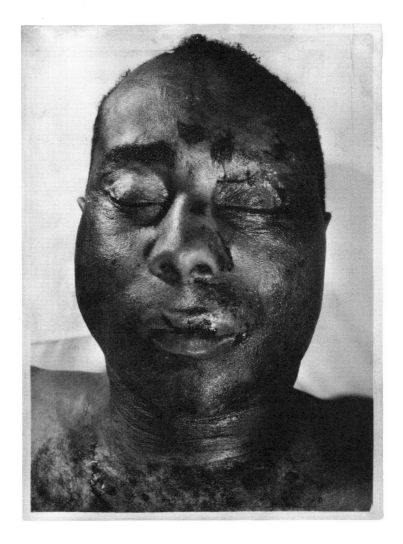

Remarkably few of us ever have real contact with the violence that fascinates us. Yet the wincing ladies who soak up true crime books and the youngsters mesmerized by slasher lore share a peculiar satisfaction with disaster survivors and the veterans of war—it's the glorious sense of "you're dead and I'm not." We feel superior to the past and to the dead. Abe Lincoln, Albert Einstein and Marilyn Monroe are all inferior to any wino bum alive today.

This book is dark for human eyes to endure. These dead have not lost their human identity no matter how desperately skewed or mutilated. Jack Huddleston's expert anger and our own mesmerized revulsion are rooted in the same fear. Fear is neither a disease nor a perversion. Fear is our most essential survival mechanism. It has many forms and functions. The mouse staring into the snake's face doesn't apologize for its interest.

They say man is the animal that knows it will die, but most days we're too deliberately stupid to fear death. We fear ways of dying. We dread pain and panic, chaos and the crushing humiliation of helplessness, the red shame of spewing bowels and bladder—the same things we fear in life. A steer in the slaughterhouse knows as much about death as we do, most days. This is a book about all those fears and the one beyond that we seldom confront.

This scrapbook of violent death is also Jack Huddleston's revenge. These are the images of

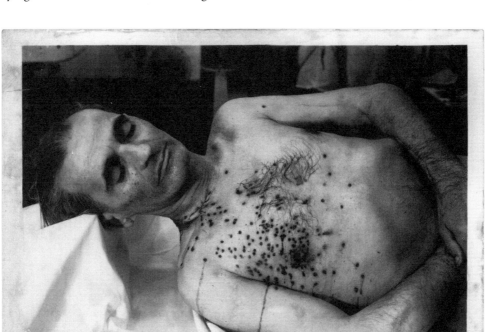

his resentment that the rest of us—the green public—can arrange our lives to avoid the sight of death, to salt it away in hospitals and darkened rooms, to sanitize it by euphemism. We can ignore and deny it through much of our lives, while he, sworn to protect and serve, must wallow in it, finger it, inhale it at a moments notice with only a hanky over the nose or a strong cigarette to screen him from the reality, not just of death but of our darkest passions and instincts run amok. He, in the suit and fedora with the long piano-player's hands, he is the garbage collector and septic pump for us all.

And if our crimes have not changed over the decades, neither have the forms of cop didacticism. Modern cops are even more defensive than Jack Huddleston, more anxious to convince us that it's a jungle out there, that the thin blue line of heroes is all that stands between us and complete mayhem. Yet the long fictional propaganda campaign to paint the police as good guys in thousands of television dramas, movies and schlock mystery books has failed. Even the most righteous citizens still fear them, profoundly and correctly. They are, after all, the biggest, most heavily armed and deadly gang in any town.

Jack Huddleston's force was the root stock of the LAPD whose current image is of another lean, plain-clothes detective, a suave perjurer on the witness stand, fueled by venomous racism to brutalize and plant false evidence against black people. This is the LAPD defined by the uniformed cops who beat an unarmed black man, and turned their backs as the riots began. This is the LAPD that presided over, and some say colluded in, the OTHER Kennedy assassination. It is the cradle of the Special Weapons Assault Tactics teams invented by Darrell Gates under the umbrella euphemism of pro-active crime fighting—a strategy which is all too often imple-

mented by cops becoming criminal themselves. The political traditions of Jack Huddleston's day

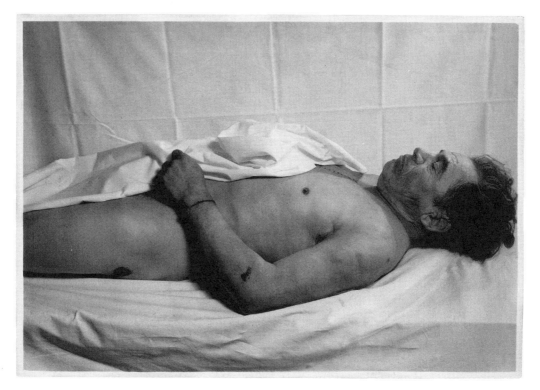

continue, with police forces driving ethnic groups into isolated pockets, exaggerating the crime rate and inflating their own levels of risk at contract renewal time.

So the scrapbook is also Jack Huddleston's confession, his plea bargain. The detective writes his little introductory rationale as the excuse, the socially redeeming purpose behind his obsession. If there is any truth in it, it is the stained white flag waved by the hostage taker. It is the "you-made-me-this-way," the "I-did-it-for-you," the "this-hurts-me-more-than-it-hurts-you" lies of the bully and abuser. The old cop, like the old con, tries to trick us into forgiveness and complicity. By witnessing he has participated, by understanding he is culpable. And his real purpose is to disguise the truth—that he started out terrified and ended up liking it, fascinated, an afficionado.

JACK HUDDLESTON
SANTA MONICA, CALIFORNIA
1921

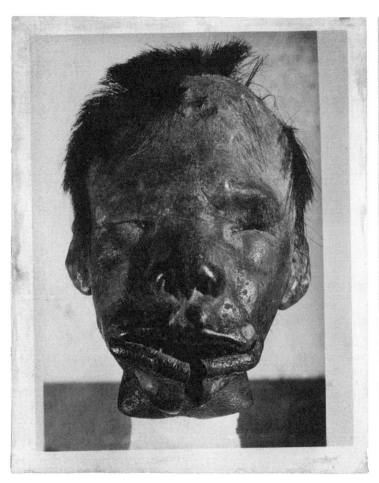 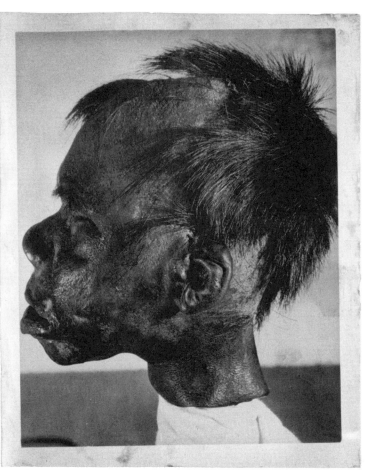

SHRUNKEN HEAD (BORNEO). 1944.

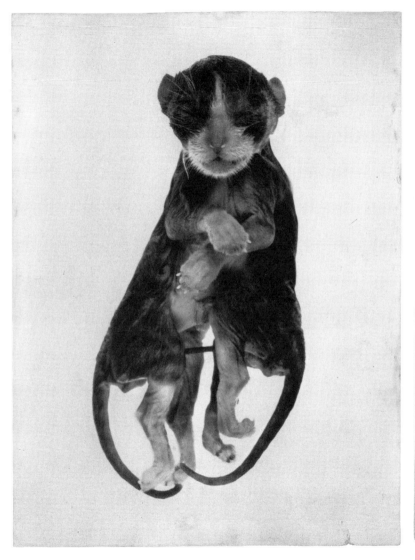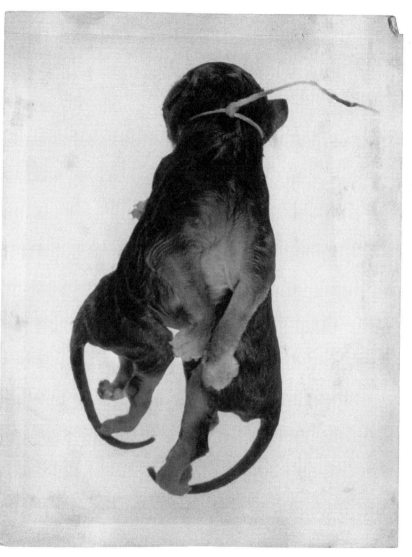

SIAMESE CATS. FRESNO. CAL.

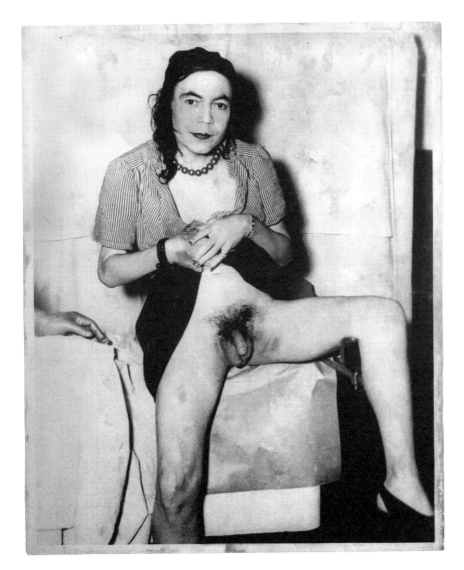

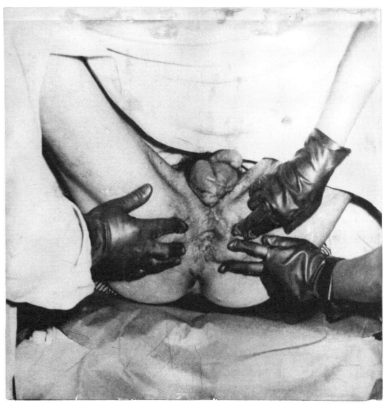

HERMAPHRODITE
MALE. & FEMALE.

HERMAPHRODITE ⟶
"MALE AND FEMALE"

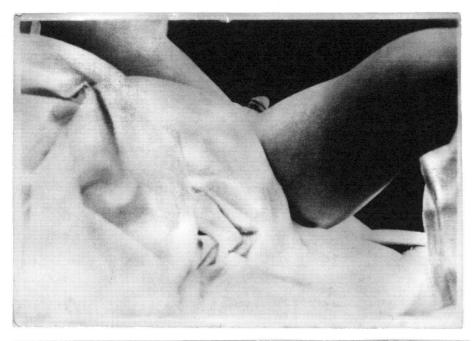

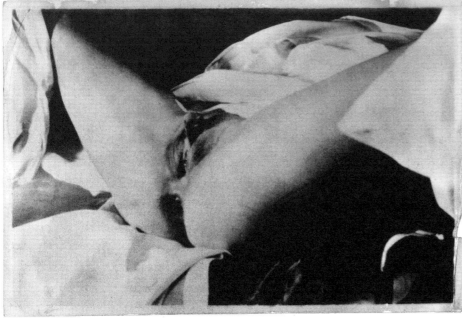

BILL BARBER & RAY HALL.
"QUEER"

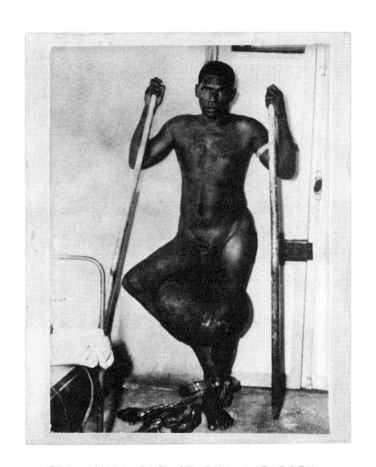

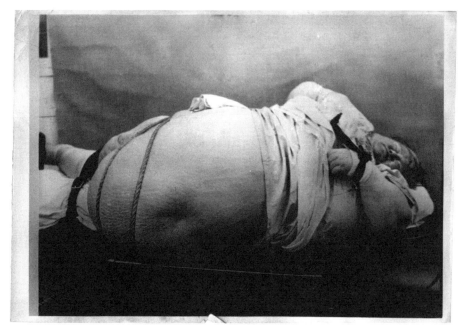

ELEPHANTIASIS OF THE TESTICLE.
SOUTH AFRICA. 1946.

ELEPHANTIASIS.

AN OBSTINATE AND CHRONIC DISEASE AFFECTING THE SKIN AND LYMPHATICS.OCCURRING CHIEFLY
IN TROPICAL COUNTRIES AND CHARACTERIZED BY AN ENORMOUS ENLARGEMENT OF THE PART AFFECTED.
GENERALLY THE LEGS AND EXTERNAL GENITALS.THE SKIN BECOMES DISCOLORED.THICKENED.AND
HARDENED.CAUSED BY MINUTE WORM LIKE PARASITES IN THE BLOOD.AND CONVEYED BY MOSQUITOES.

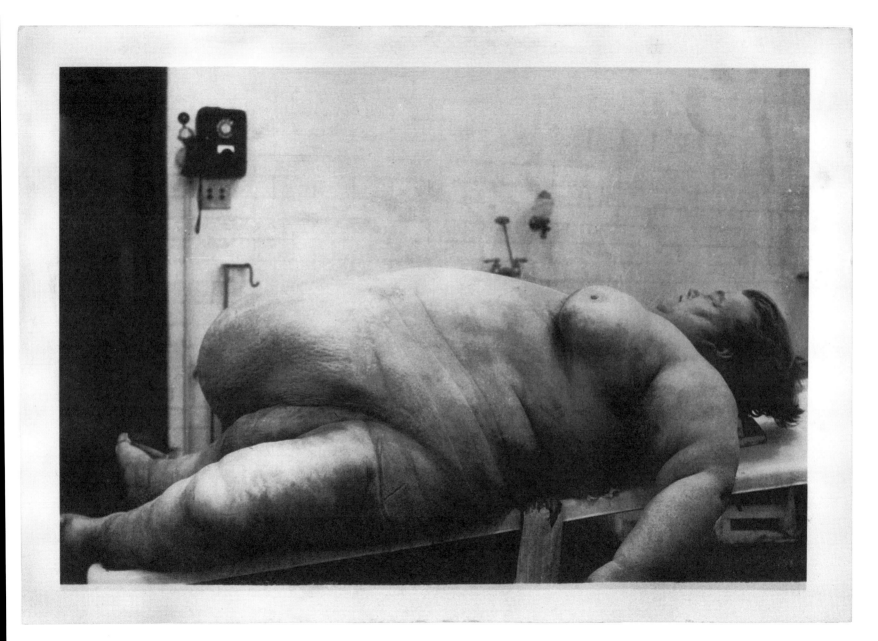

ELEPHANTIASIS

EXHIBITIONIST.

Ben Johnson arrested 8-28-43,L.A,on a moral charge.He wore an overcoat and would flash the front for the women,and the rear for the men ,Re-leased 9-2-43.

FOR SALE $800 00
NEW YORK CHINATOWN 1908.
ROWS OF CAGES WERE ON EXHIBIT
AND SOLD TO THE HEIGHEST BIDDER.
"WHITE SLAVERY"

FRANCOIS. DE. LA. MARIE. 52, YEARS.
VAGRANCY. & DISTURBING THE PEACE.
HE HAD LEWD PICTURES TATTOOED FROM
HEAD TO FOOT. (IN, COLOR) ALSO PICTURES
SHOWING HIM IN THE NUDE, EXHIBITING
HIS TATTOOS.

?

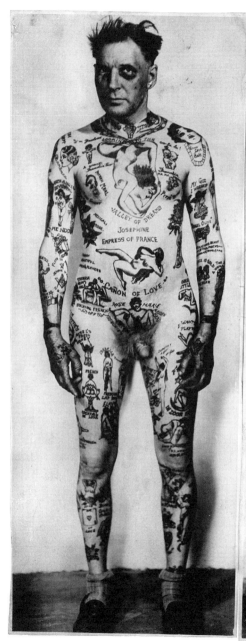

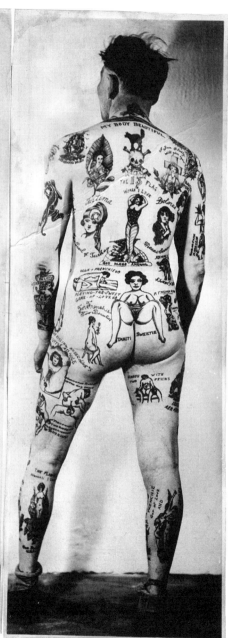

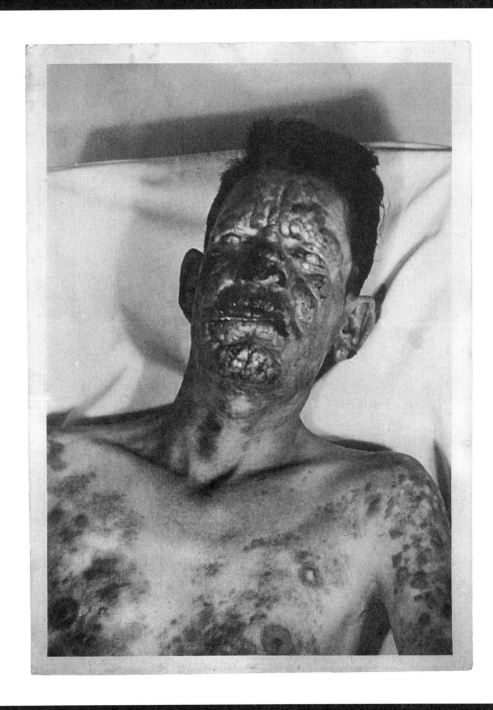

LEPROSY. L.A. COUNTY HOSPITAL.

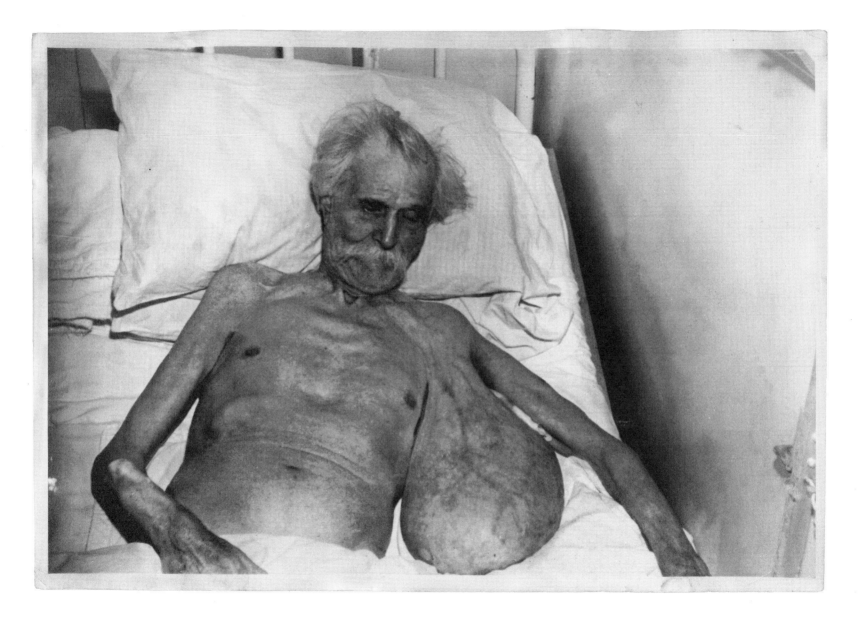

"WEN" A MOVABLE, TUMOR   AGE 95 YRS.   L.A. COUNTY HOSPITAL.

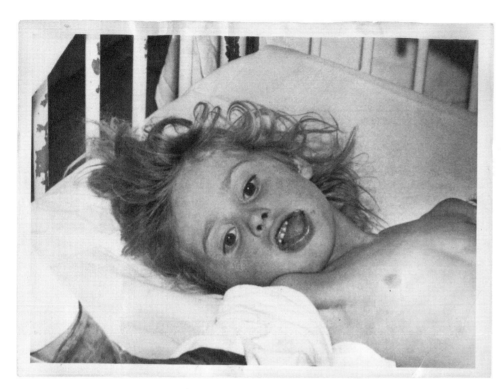 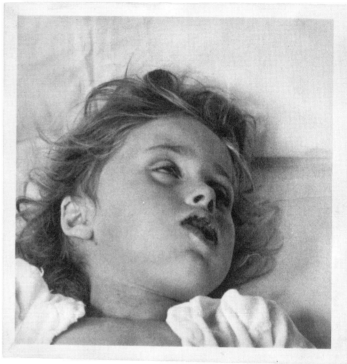

ALIVE.   HYDROPHOBIA.   DEATH.

A DISEASE COMMUNICATED BY THE BITE OF A RABID ANIMAL,DUE TO A SPECIFIC VIRUS IN THE SALIVA,CHARACT-
ERIZED BY GREAT DISTURBANCE OF THE CENTRAL NERVOUS SYSTEM,DIFFICULTY OF SWALLOWING,CONVULSIVE DREAD
OF WATER,AND SPASMODIC MUSCULAR CONTRACTIONS.IN HYDROPHOBIA THERE ARE THREE STAGES.IN THE FIRST,THE
PREMONITORY STAGE,THERE ARE PAIN AND IRRITATION IN THE VICINITY OF THE BITE,AND THE VICTIM BECOMES
DEPRESSED.IN THE SECOND,THE STAGE OF EXCITEMENT,WHICH LASTS FROM ONE TO FOUR DAYS,CONVULSIONS SET
IN AND A VISCID SECRETION COLLECTS IN THE THROAT.THE CHOKING COUGH,WHICH RESEMBLES THE "BARKING OF
A DOG",IS MERELY THE EFFORT TO CLEAR THE THROAT OF THE MUCOUS SECRETION,AND NOT AS FORMERLY THOUGHT,
AN ATTEMPT AT BARKING.IN THE THIRD,THE PARALYTIC STAGE,UNCONSCIOUSNESS BEGINS AND DEATH OCCURS.
LOUIS PASTEUR A FRENCH CHEMIST ADVANCED THE SCIENCE IN THE TREATMENT FOR RABIES.

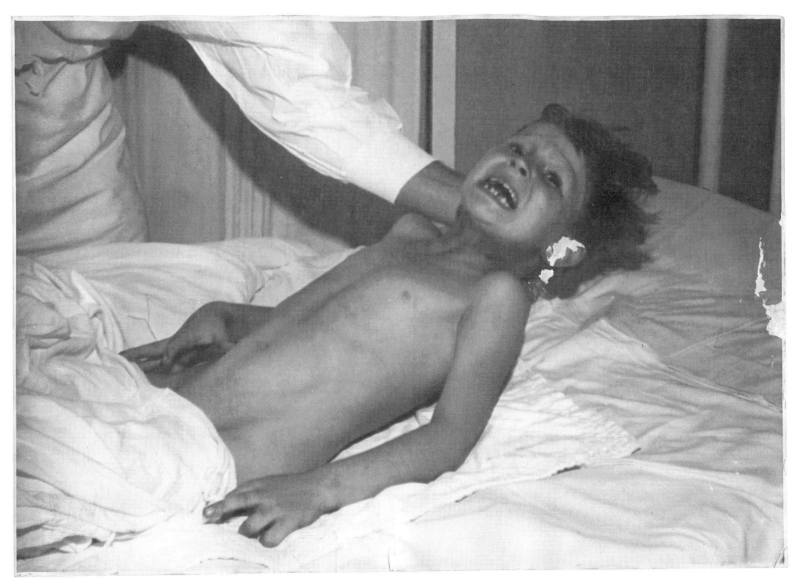

HYDROPHOBIA

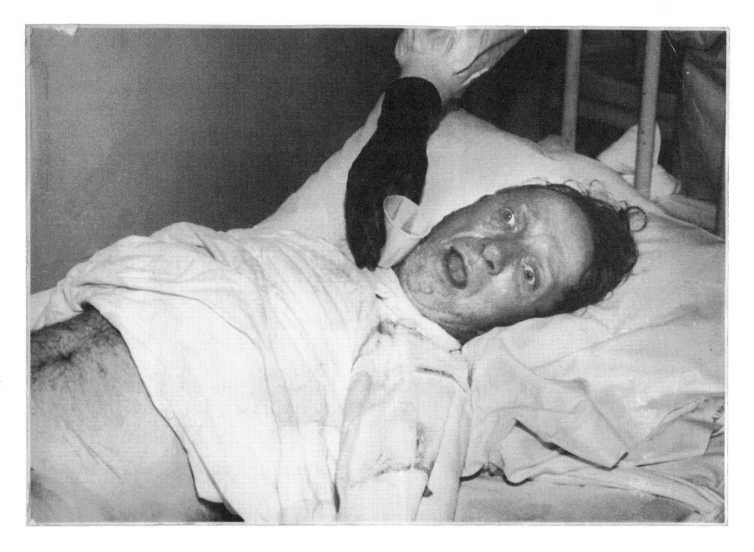

HYDROPHOBIA

ATTEMPT SUICIDE, LOCKJAW,
ARM AMPUTATED. "GUN"

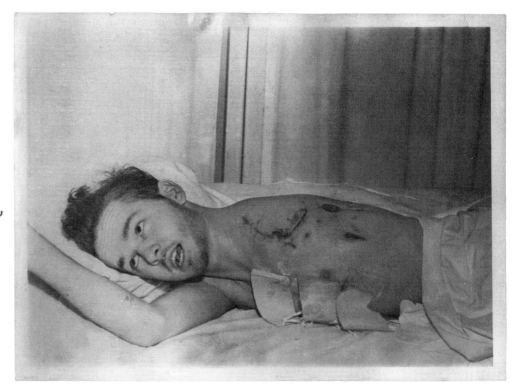

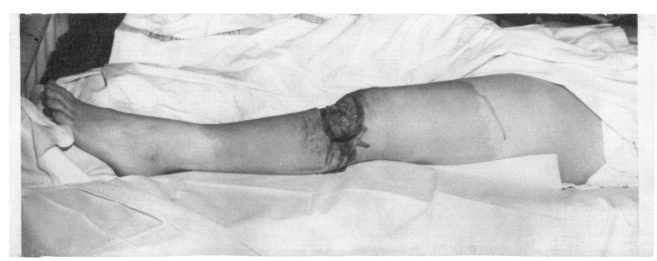

LOCKJAW

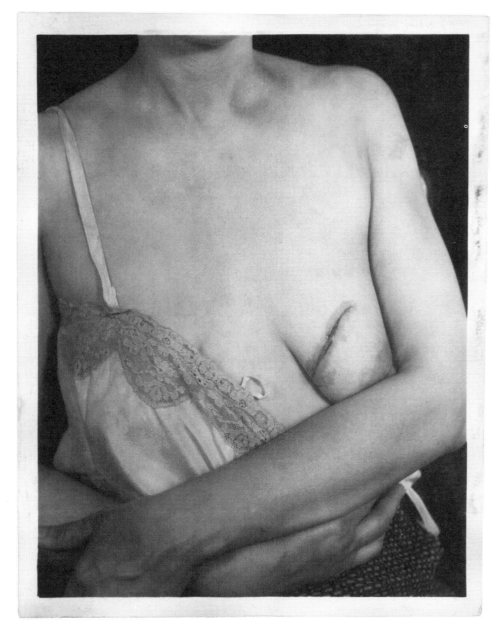

FIGHT

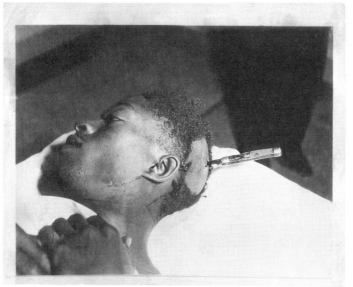

FIGHT "LIVING"

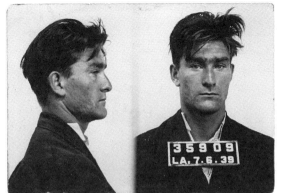

BUNCO.

CON-MAN.

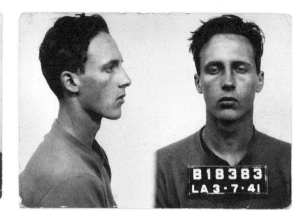

SAFE BLOWER.

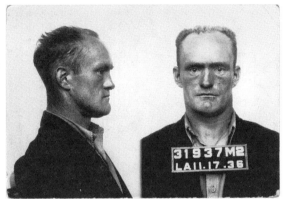

KIDNAPING.

THESE PORTRAIT'S ARE "NOT" BY, REMBRANDT.

MURDER

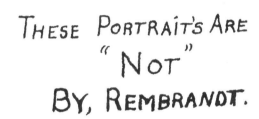

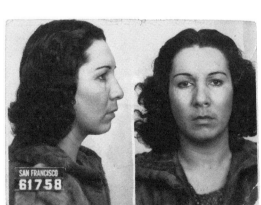

MURDER

THEFT FROM PERSON

MENTAL CASE.

HOLD UP.

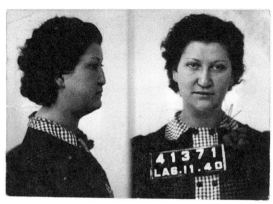

A.D.W. GUN.

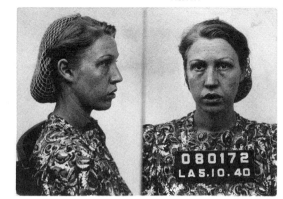

MENTAL CASE.

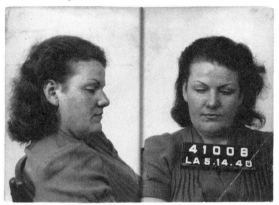

BADGER. GAME.

EMBEZZLEMENT.

LESBIAN.

PROSTITUTE.

PROCURESS.

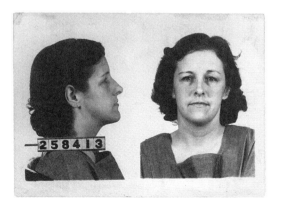

BURG AND THEFT

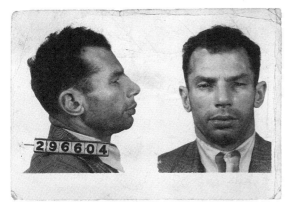

MURDER S.Q.

IND EXP.

A.D.W. KNIFE.

BAD CHECKS.

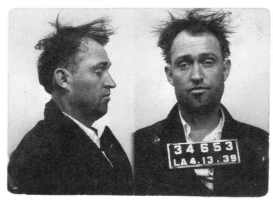

DRUNK "AUTO" HIT + RUN.

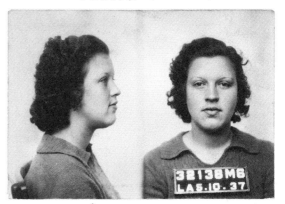

CHILD NEGLECT.

A.D.W. GUN.

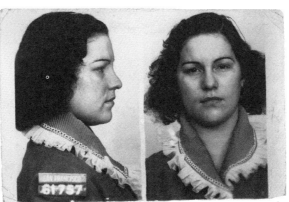

SHOP LIFTER.

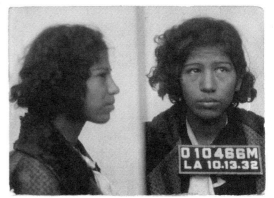

"SALE" MARIJUANA.

STOLEN CAR. & ROBBERY

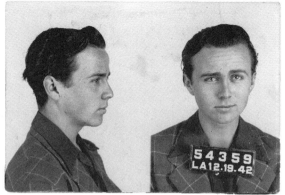

ATTACK "SEX"

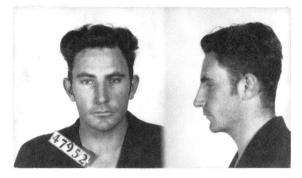

HOLD UP

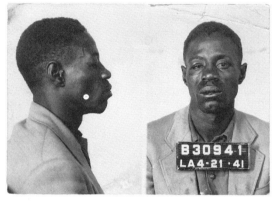

A.D.W. CUTTING "RAZOR"

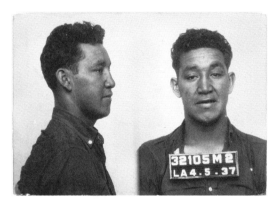

"ROBBERY" STRONG ARMED MAN.

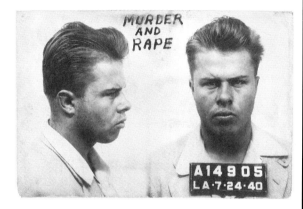

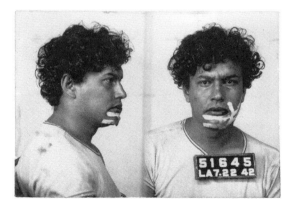

MENTAL CASE.

GRAND LARCENY, AUTO.

SAFE BLOWER.

HOLD UP.

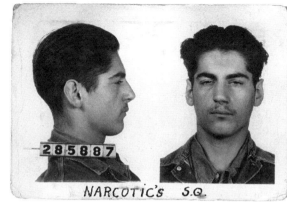

NARCOTIC'S S.Q.

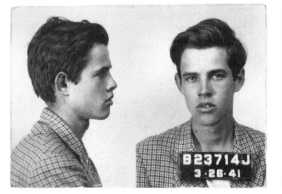

SMUGGLING OPIUM.

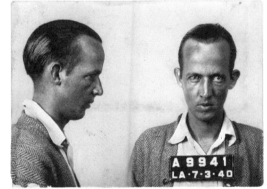

FORGERY.

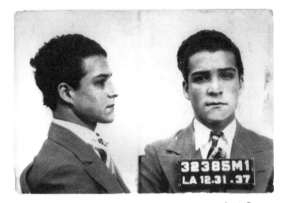

SODOMY AND CARNAL ABUSE.

PIMP † C.C.W. GUN

PICKPOCHET.

ARSON

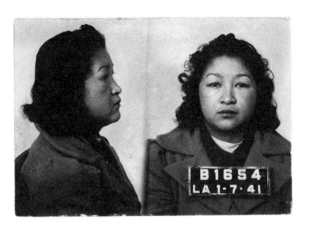

PRESILLA TAYLOR.

VERNON WOODWARD.

PROSTITUTES AND ROBBERY.

~~THOSE WHO ADDED THE TWO MANITIPLIERS.~~

STINK BOMBS. 375

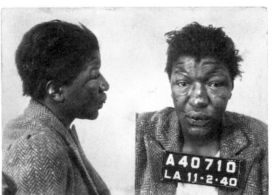

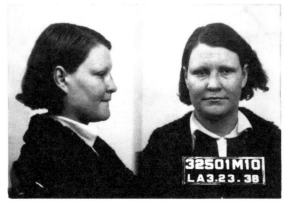

LESBIAN "DEBAUCHERY"

HOLD UP. & BAD CHECKS.

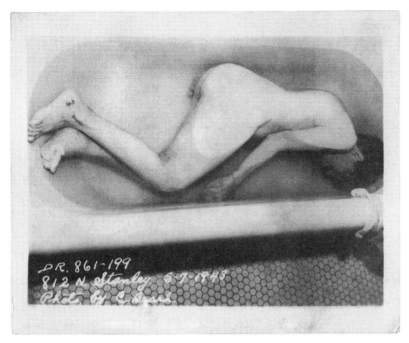

DR. 861-199
812 N. Stanley 5-7-1943
Photo by C. Opal

DR 785 479
6-28-42 OLIVER

VICTOR WHEALAND, FELL A SLEEP IN THE BATH TUB
AND DROWNED, 4477, HOLLYWOOD BLVD. L.A.

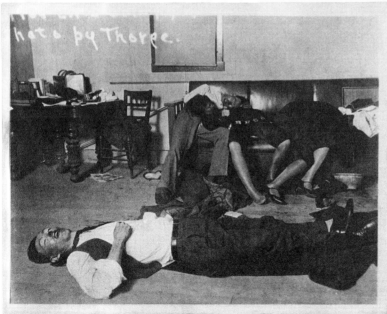

Photo by Thorpe.

DRUNKEN PARTY. OVER COME
BY MONOX GAS. WATTS CAL.

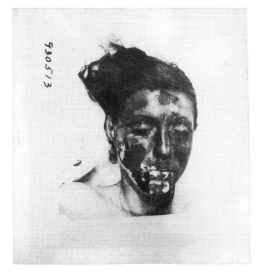
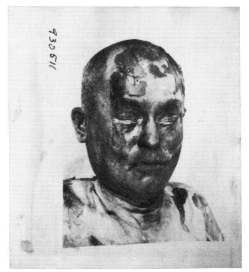
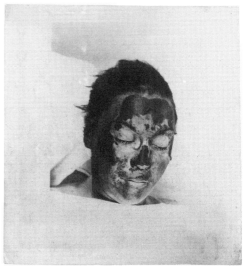

Left to right,Clarebel Wimmer age 26.Lois Johnson age 26.John Rueter age 65,Killed in an explosion at Noll & Co manufacturers of dice and gaming equipment,at 2030 Wilshire Blvd. L,A,Calif.9-13-43.Norman Noll owner did not use proper fire precautions,

"24 MEN" GRIFFITH P.K. FIRE.
1936 L.A. CAL.

MISS MARAVENE TERRY BURNED TO DEATH CAUSED
BY SMOKING A CIGARETTE IN BED. 1922 NO
HIGHLAND AVE APT 16, 12-19-42.

EXPLOSION DYNAMITE.
Boy on left and Girl on right found some dynamite near one of our dams.
It exploded in their hands, No names or dates as it is unsolved by F B I.

Photo by C. S. Myers

TWO KILLED, "HIT AND RUN"
THIS BOY'S TOE WAS IN HIS SHOE
100 FT FROM THE BODY. L.A. Co.

ONE KILLED L.A. Co   TWO KILLED, FRESNO. CAL

AUTO ACCIDENT FRESNO CAL.

AEROPLANE ACCIDENT.

HIT AND RUN.

DRIVER AND TWO PAS. UN-HURT. L.A.Co.

THE BODY

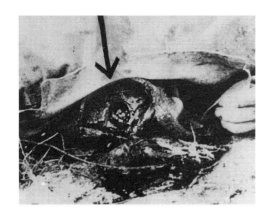

SHOWING IMAGE
OF HEAD IN THE NECK.

OVERTURNED AUTO WITH BODY AND
HEAD DECAPITATE'D.

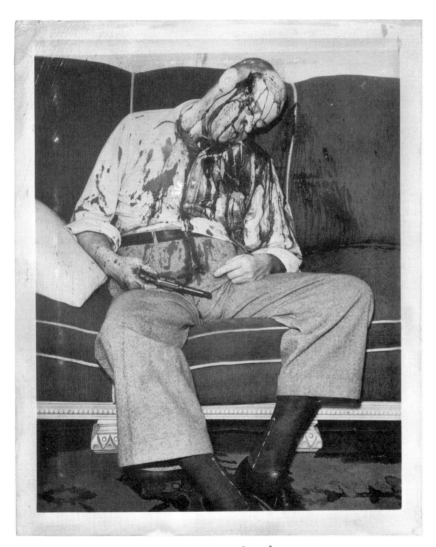

WM. H. LOVETT SUICIDE 7-4-37.
L.A.

S
U
I
C
I
D
E

SUICIDE.
ANT POISON AND KNIFE.
3-12-41 L.A.

FRANK E O'TOOLE KILLED HIS COMMON LAW WIFE,
LILLIAN WHITE WITH A GUN WHILE SHE WAS
SLEEPING,HE WAS STANDING IN COURT AS THE
JUDGE SENTENCED HIM TO DEATH HE JUMPED OUT
OF THE WINDOW.9-29-42.

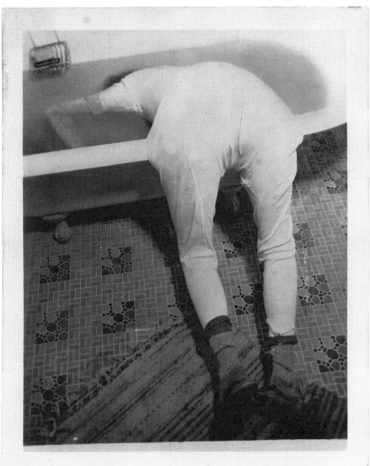

JOE MARTIN SUICIDE 4-21-37
BATH.TUB.   L.A.

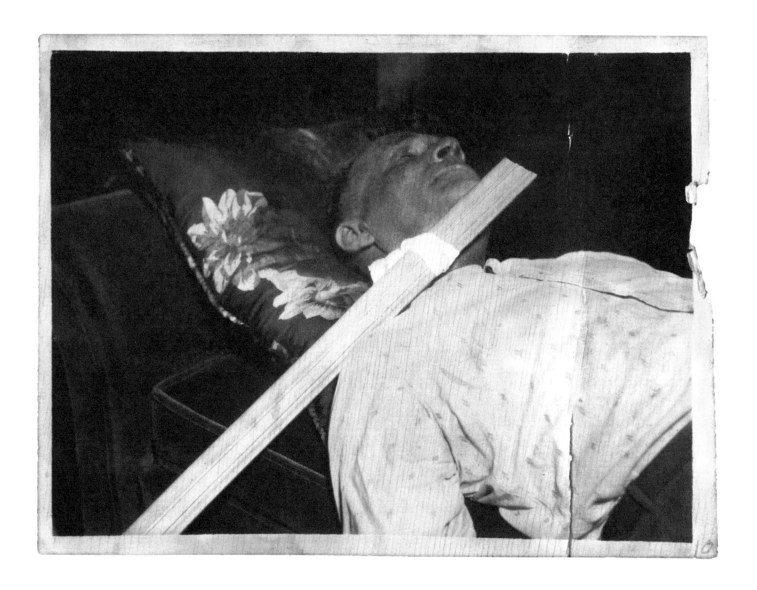

SUICIDE   SANTA MONICA CAL.

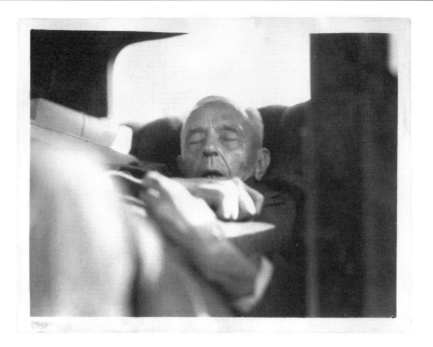

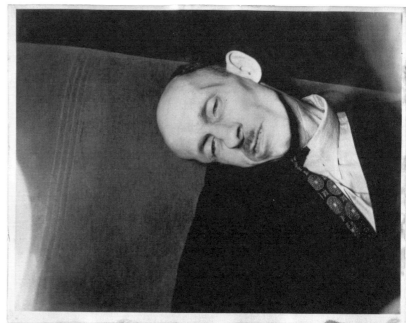

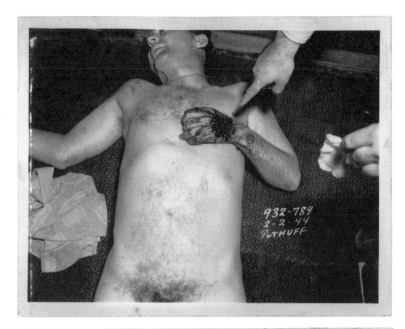

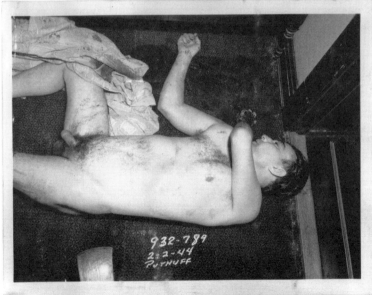

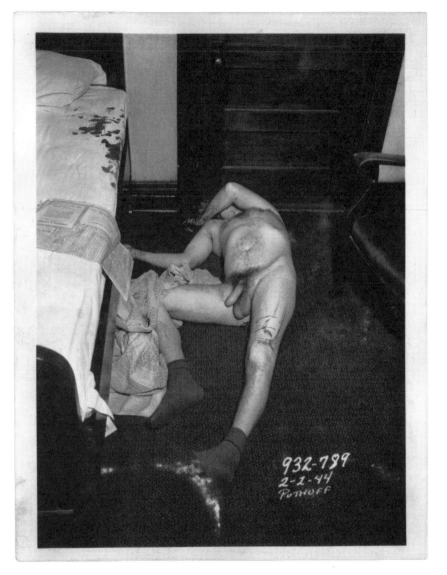

← SUICIDE MONOX GAS

Sgt Lloyd L,Evans,Flyer U,S,Army.age 37.
Suicide cut on back of left hand with razor.
No motive,very drunk,room 263,Rosslyn Hotel.
4PM 2-2-44,L,A,Calif.

FRANK HI 'CHCLIFF

ING MACHINE 8-23-31

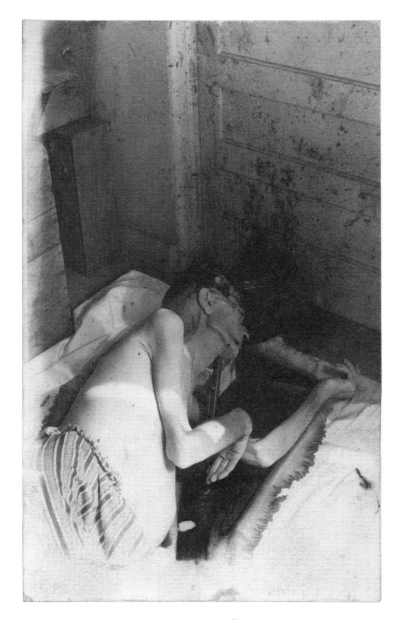

SUICIDE, SHOTGUN
.SANTA MONICA CAL.

Ralph Redlyn Suicide 631 Ventura St.
Tulare Calif.

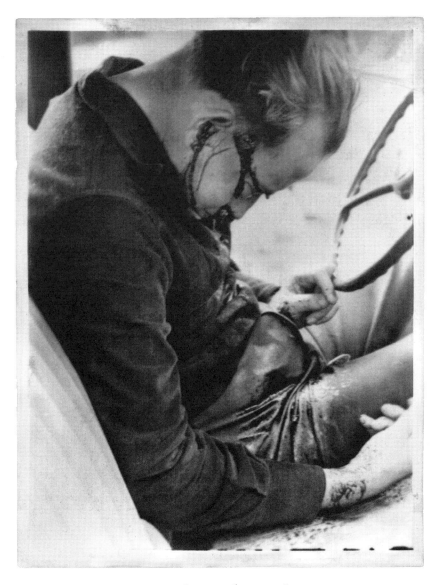

SUICIDE

SUICIDE "GUN"

PAT GORMAN "SUICIDE" DENATURED, ALC.

SUICIDE.

SUICIDE 15 YRS OLD
CAUSED BY
A BROKEN HOME, AND
A BROKEN HEART.

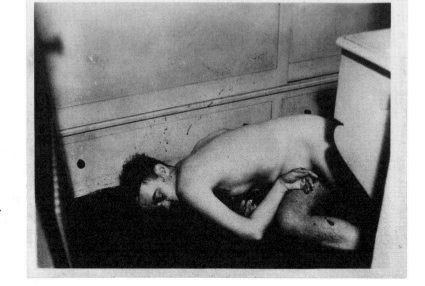

PAUL BERN JEAN HARLOW HUSBAND.
SUICIDE. "GUN"
?

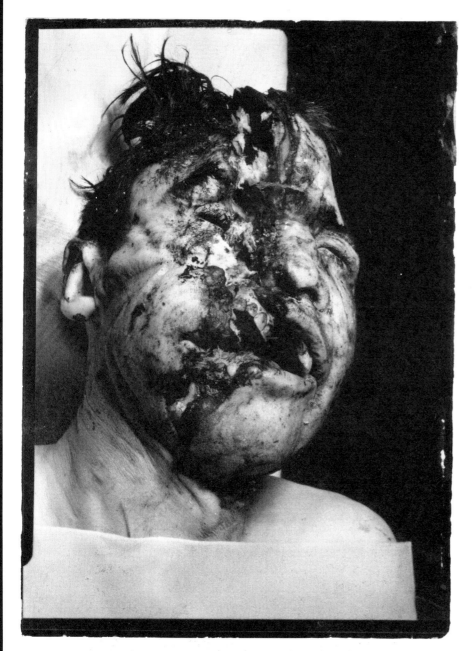

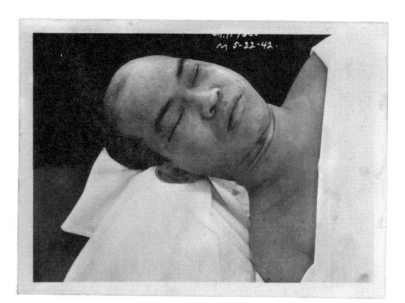

SUICIDE.

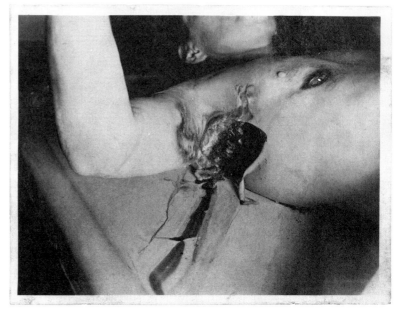

SUICIDE SHOT GUN

SUICIDE SHOT GUN

SUICIDE

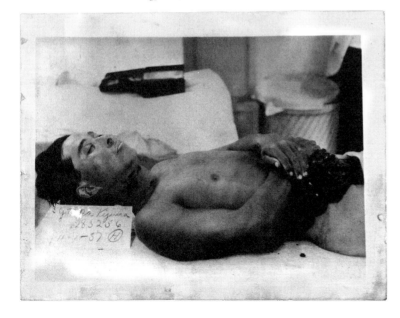

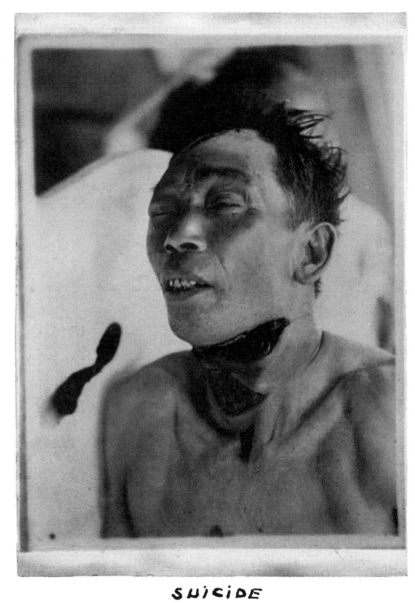

SUICIDE

HARA-KARI JAP SUICIDE

JUST A LITTLE
THROAT TROUBLE

290·837
1-4-47
G.C.B.

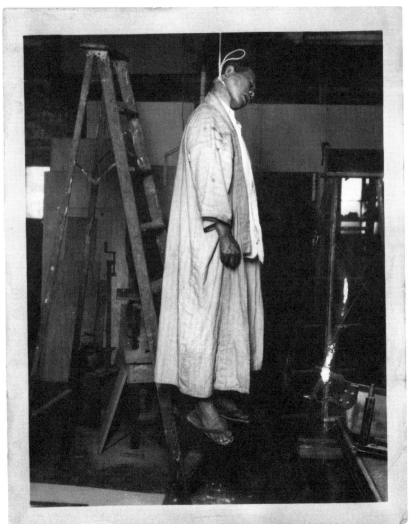

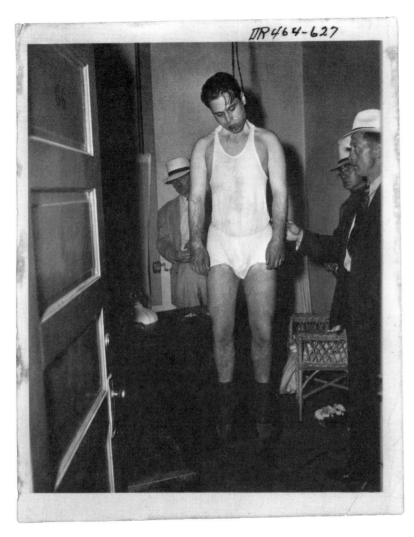

DR464-627

DR.861-199   5-7-1943
812 N. Stanley
Photo by C. Beard

HERB COHAN, COMMITED SUICIDE BY HANGING.
IN HIS OFFICE. R.K.O. STUDIO HOLLYWOOD.
JUNE 1939.

 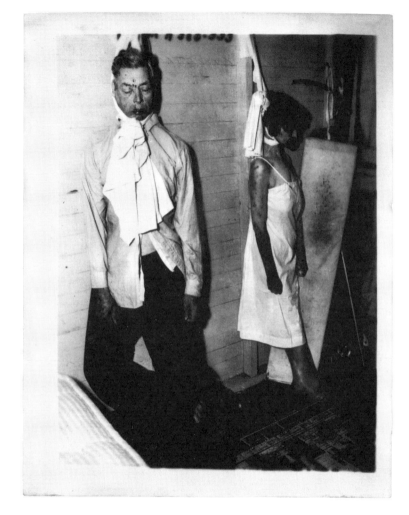

MURIAL MORRISON AGE 58

FRED MORRISON AGE 69 YRS HELPED HIS WIFE TO HANG HERSELF
LIVED IN THE HOUSE TWO DAYS BEFORE HANGING HIMSELF 6-27-40
1001½ No MARIPOSA ST L.A. CAL.

THEY KILLED HER BABY THEN KILLED EACH OTHER "JAPS" 4-2-29. L.A. CAL

WHELOCK HUBBELL, SUICIDE
WITH HOME MADE SHOT GUN
COMPOSED OF PIPE AND NAIL
STRUCK WITH HAMMER.
L.A.Co. 11-30-32.

D.R.#A-15517
PHOTO by HOWATT
2-12-'35

Suicide he used two Shot-Guns.
L,A,Calif,2/12/35.

E.L.Doheny Jr shot and killed his secretary
Bill Plunkett(body in the hall)then commited
suicide.Beverly Hills Cal.

COY TOWNSEND KILLED GEO MC NEAL "TOP
PHOTO" WITH A SHOT GUN, THEN COMMITED
SUICIDE. NOTE SKULL AND BRAINS ON
PORCH. L.A. CAL.

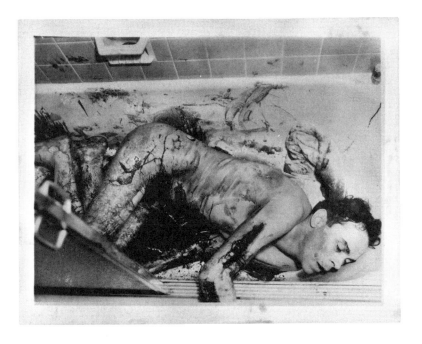

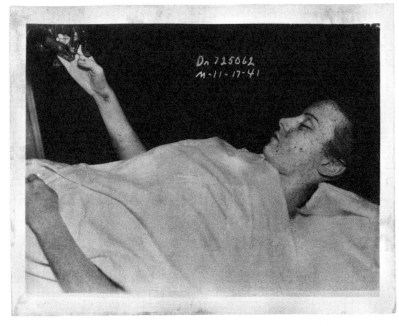

Dn 725062
M-11-17-41

MURDER AND SUICIDE.

Dr Stuart E,Noland gave his wife
(Kay Pengra Noland)a Hypodermic,
cut her wrist,combed her hair,put
a Jade Plaque on her,then got in
the bath tub and commited suicide.
8963 Burton Way Hollywood Calif,
II/I5/4I.

DR A 420-232   DR A 420-232

ARTHUR FULLER ESTELLE GREEN
SUICIDE AND MURDER.
1-26-39

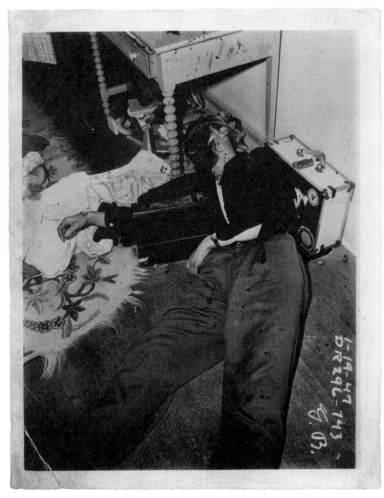

Mrs Georgiana Sokol age 27.Killed by her discharged
overseas husband,Julius F.Sokol age 29.He came home
and found his wife living with Joseph Oliver age 28.
He killed them,then he commited suicide.4422 Prospect Ave.
Los Angeles Calif,I2-I7-45.

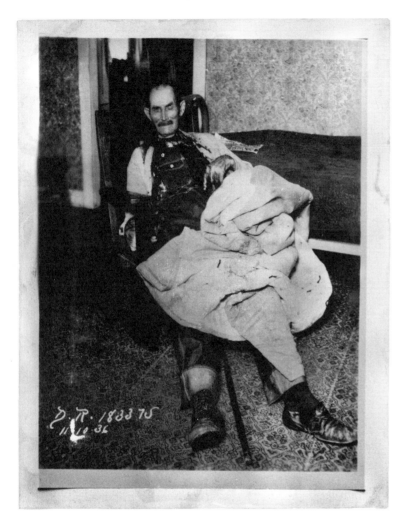

Charles Johnson age 91 killed by
his wife Anna age 83, she cut his
throat while he was a sleep in a
chair & then hanged her self.
Motive Jealousy, She saw him
talking to a neighbour woman.
L,A,Calif.II/10/36.

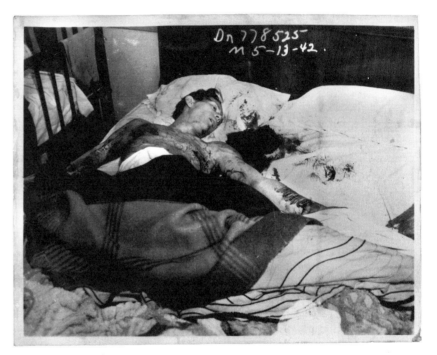

EARL BLAISURE KILLED BY HIS GIRL FRIEND.
SHE STUCK A 7 IN KNIFE IN HIS CHEST
THEN SLASHED HIS WRIST'S 1030 DOCTURE ST.
L. A.

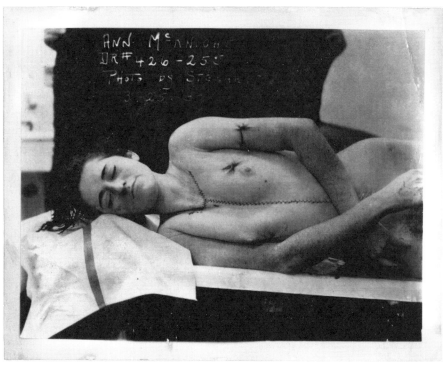

Ann McKnight killed by her husband Wm H Burkhart,He took her body to a vacent bungalow on Franklin Place Hollywood,Raped & committed Sodomy on the body which was on the floor. Then dragged her face up by the feet through the house and out towards his car.Arrested just as he reached the sidewalk.Hanged S,Q,3/24/30.

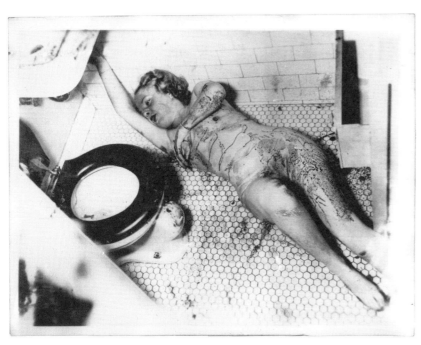

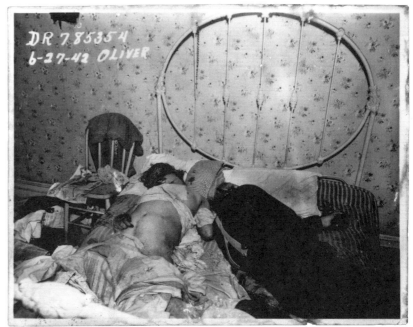

VANTHALIA McCANDLESS
KILLED BY HER HUSBAND

MARY E RICKARD KILLED BY HER HUSBAND.
HE WAS DRUNK IN THE ROOM FOR FIVE DAYS.
WITH THE BODY. "NOTE" MAGGOTS. "EXONERATED"
221 E 12TH ST RM 12 LA. CAL. 6-27-42.

FRED OESTERREICH KILLED IN HIS HOME.

OTTO SANHUBER
alias WALTER KLEIN

PHANTOM OF THE ATTIC MURDER.

Otto Sanhuber was a secret lover of Mrs Dolly Oesterreich he lived in
the attic of their home for Nine Years at 858 No St Andrews Pl,L,A,
with out her husband Fred knowing it.When Dolly would entertain the
Ice-man,Butcher,and Milk-man,Otto would go to his room in the attic
where he had a peep-hole into Dolly bedroom.Otto Sanhuber shot and
killed Fred Oesterreich for quarreling with Dolly,8-22-1922.Arrested
4-17-1930.Acquitted.

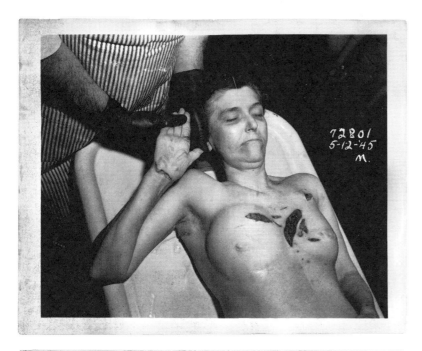

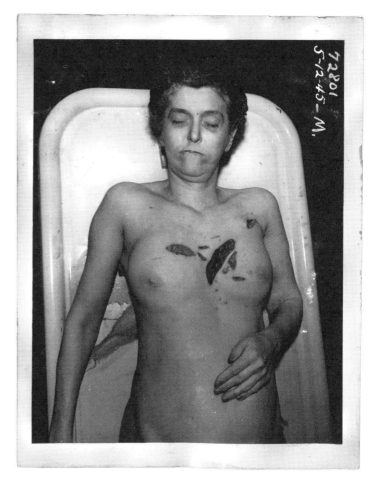

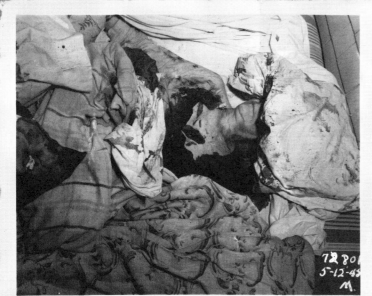

MRS MAUD ADAMS AGE 54 STABBED TO DEATH 21
TIMES BY HER 17 YEAR OLD DAUGHTER BARBARA
ADAMS A CITY COLLEGE CO-ED.PURCHASING THE
KNIFE MORE THAN 12 HOURS BEFORE THE DEED &
PRACTICING ITS EFFICIENCY BY CUTTING OFF
TWO LIVE CANARIES HEADS IN THE KITCHEN OF
THEIR HOME.SHE THAN CREPT INTO HER MOTHERS
BEDROOM TO MAKE HER SAVAGE ATTACK AT 917.
WEST 9th ST L.A.CALIF.5/12/45.MOTIVE---?
ADJUDGED INSANE.

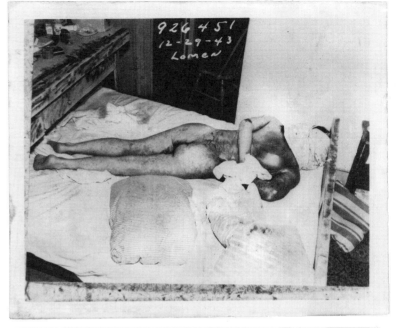

WALL BED MURDER.
Jerome 6 Hanse(Queer)Killed by Pvt
James Richmond 7II So Westlake Ave,
L,A,Cal,I2-27-43. *20 YEARS*

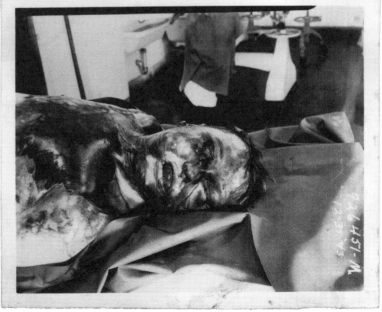

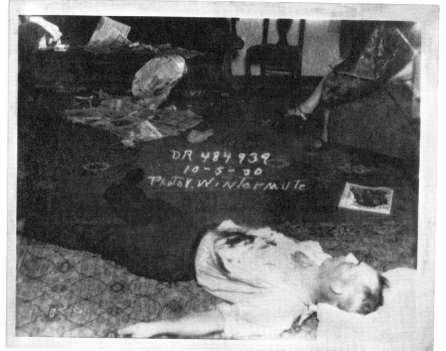

DR 484 939
10-5-30
Photo. Wintermute

KILLED BY HIS WIFE.

TOM BAY MOVIE COWBOY KILLED
BY HIS GIRL FRIEND, BURBANK CAL
(EX. CON.)

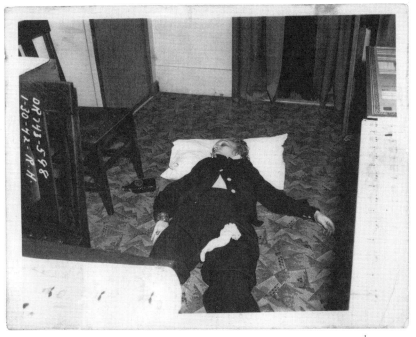

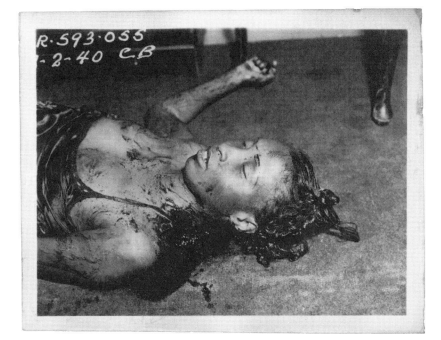

CELESTE FRANK. ALIAS. MADAM LORRAIN.
SHOT. BY CHARLOTTE LE NORD 1-30-42.
4384 SUNSET BLVD L.A. "LESBIANS"

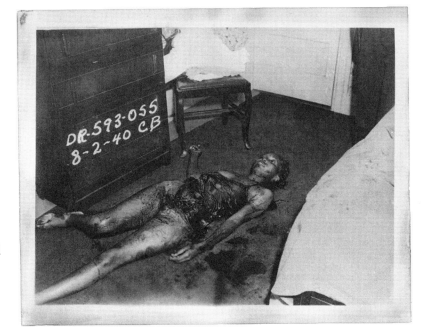

Carrie Ackerson negress age 35 shot & killed
by Mrs Lucretia McCleod negress motive
jealousy. 5 yrs to life L,A,Calif, 8/3/40.

MRS. LOLITA DAVIS AGE 36 YRS KILLED HER
THREE CHILDREN WITH A HAMMER THEN
COMMITED SUICIDE 1211 W 58 PL. L.A. 4-4-40
CHLOE DAVIS AGE 11 YRS LIVED.

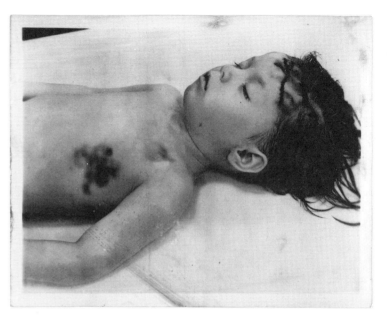

DAPHNE DAVIS

MARQUIS DAVIS AGE 3YRS

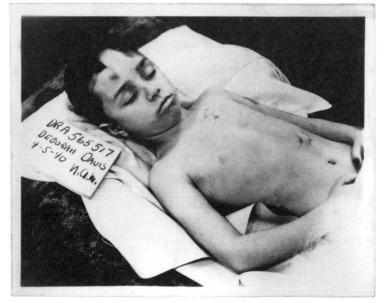

DEBORAH DAVIS

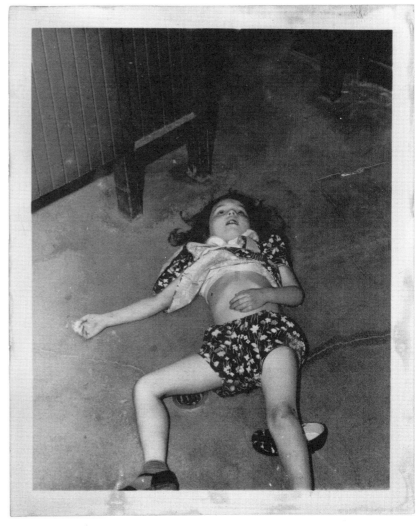

GERALDINE HARDAKER AGE 5YRS KILLED BY HER ⁴⁻⁴⁰
MOTHER "BETTY" IN PARK WASHROOM MONTEBELLO, CAL
SHE WAS RELEASED BY JUDGE RUBEN SCHMIDT
"WITHOUT STRINGS" 2-19-41. SHE WAS BACK.
IN THE SANITARIUM: 4-41. "INSANE" 7-18-41
SHE DISAPPEARED FROM WHITTIER. SANITARIUM.

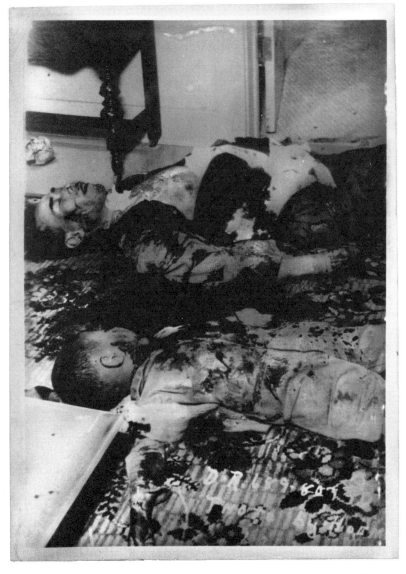

KUNIDO SAWADA   MURDER + SUICIDE BY STABBING.
"SON"   7-12-32.

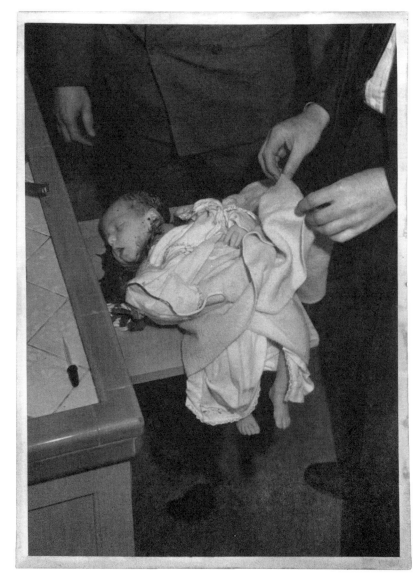

Mrs Rosary Shelfo put her two weeks
old son,on the bread board and cut
his head off,with a butcher knife.
914 East 79th St,L A Cal,3-8-43.

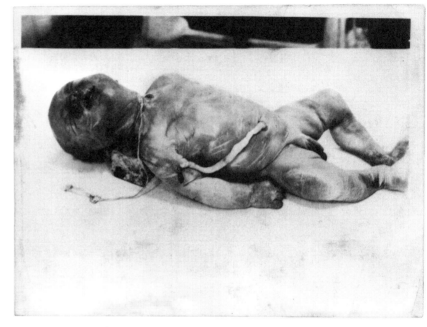

Body of male new born child washed ashore in Venice 2-21-44. Apparently thrown in ocean while still alive, according to water content in lungs. Possibly twin of female child found in same locality following day.

"MURDER" STRANGLED.
PUT IN A TRASH BARREL.

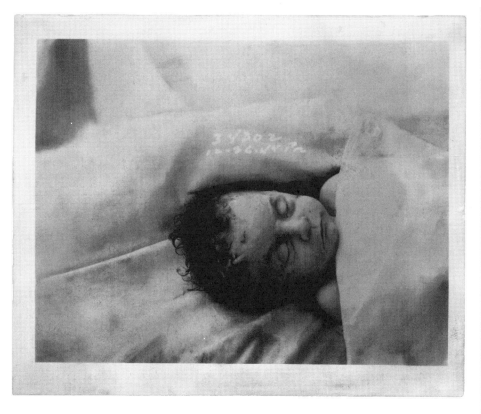

Mrs Marion Johnson age 34,threw her month
old son Earl from the 11th story window of
a building at 210 West 7TH St L.A.Calif.
12/22/44.(Motive she said he looked like
his father) ADJUDGED INSANE 1-4-45.

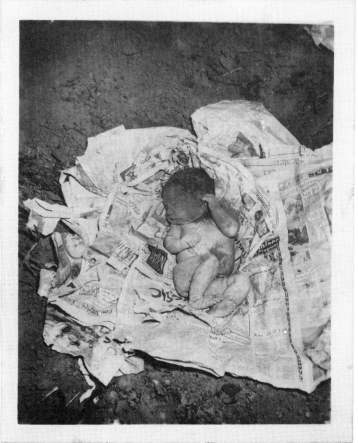

BABY. KILLED. BY MOTHER. ALBERTA
ESTES. 7-24-33-

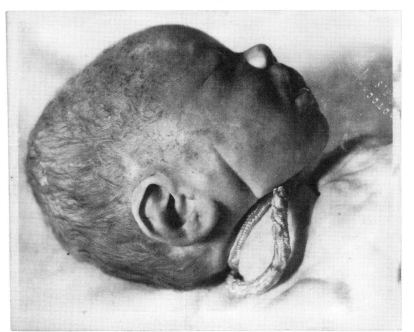

"MURDER" STRANGLED WITH A LAMP CORD
THEN PUT IN A GRIP. BY MOTHER.
MRS. C.O. ALLEXANDER. (LIFE)

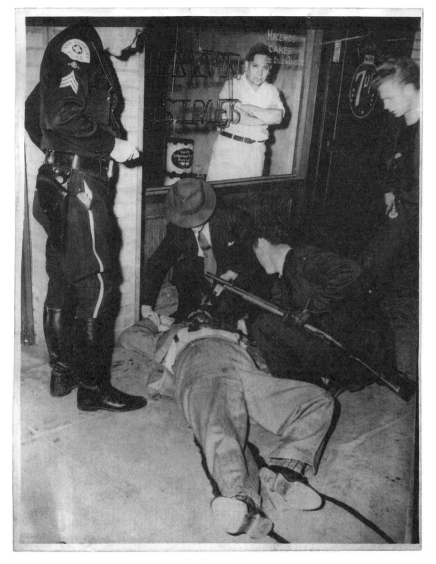

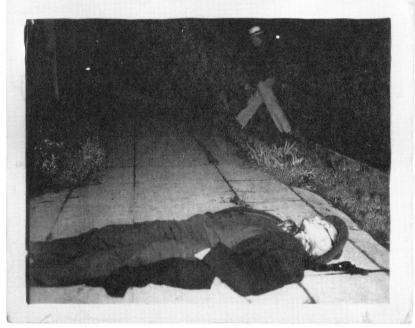

U.S. DEP MARSHALL RAOUL KILLED BY
Wᵐ PIERCE, OAKLAND CAL. 11-25-37.

Detective Lieut,Mario V Deiro,
Killed by Frank Barredas on
No Main St,New Years Eve
L.A.I-I-43 Barredas sentenced
to S,Q, I TO 10 YRS.

GEO FARLEY "NEGRO" KILLER OF DEP' MARSHALLS T.D. CRITTENDEN AND L. ROMER.

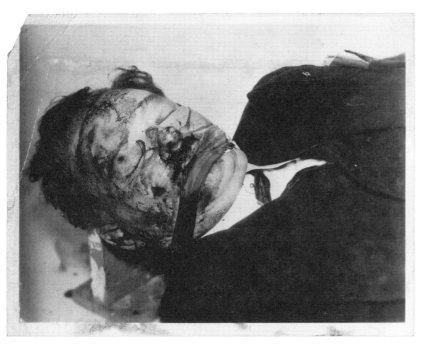

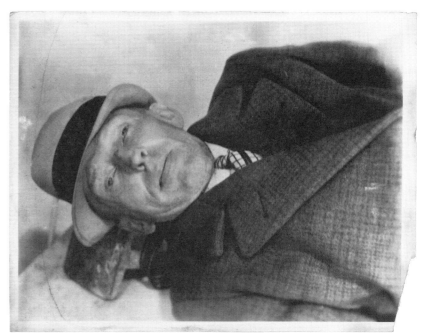

KILLED BY BANDIT

"SAME" BANDIT KILLED BY POLICE

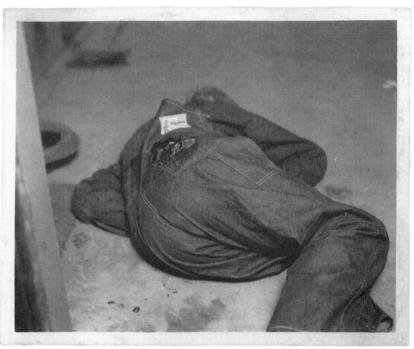

W. A. HORTON KILLED BY ELEVEN YR. OLD BANDIT

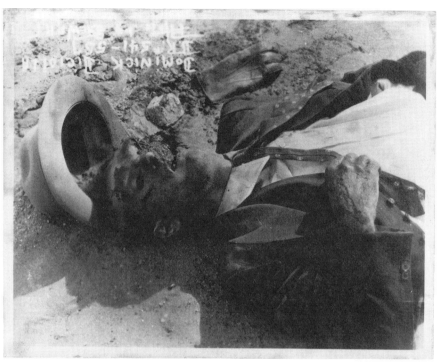

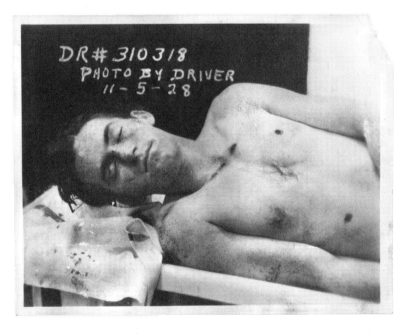

BOOTLEG MURDER

KENNITH GARISSON KILLED BY VICE.

BOOTLEG MURDER. L.A.

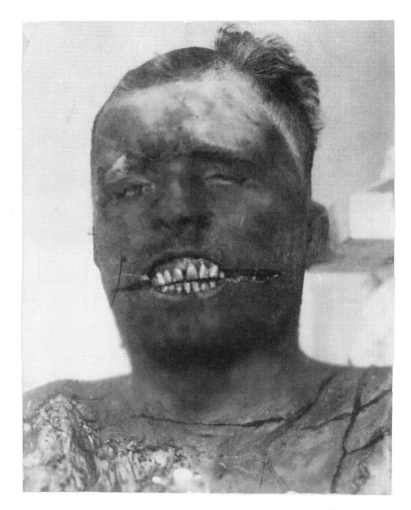

FIRST MAN TO BE TAKEN FOR A RIDE
CHICAGO
THEY CUT HIS TONGUE OFF.

3-21-31
JIM BASILE BOOTLEG SHOOTING

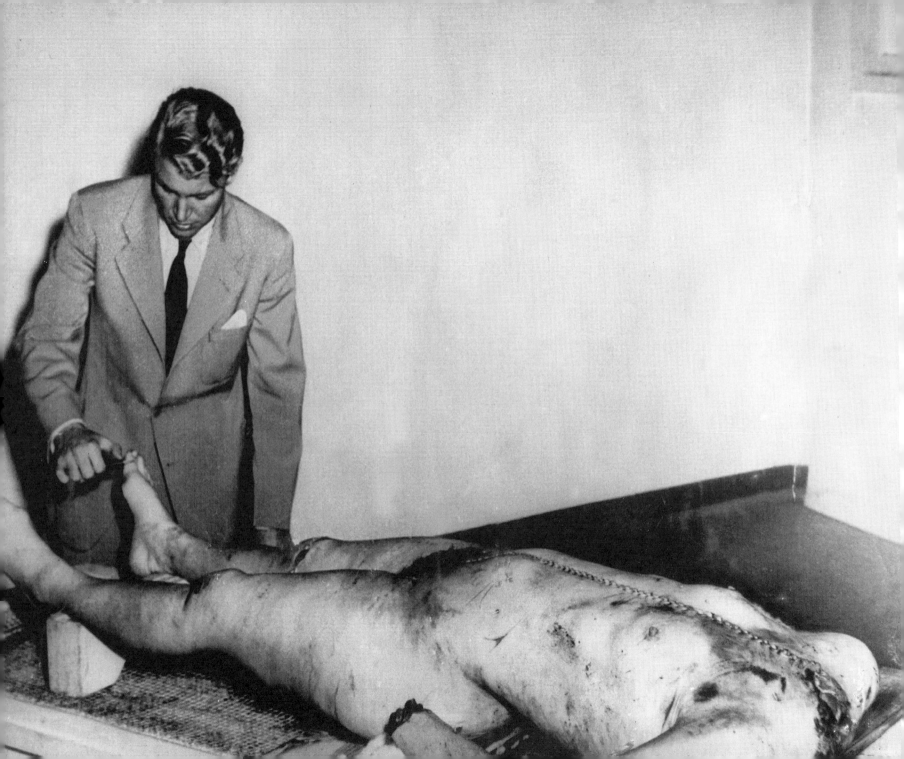

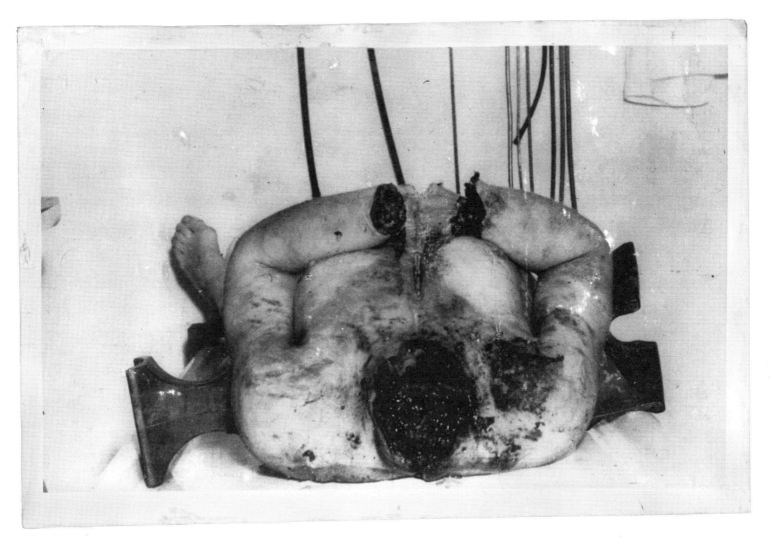

TORSO OF MRS DOROTHY LEE EGGERS AGE 41.HER DISMEMBERED BODY WAS
FOUND IN WATERMAN CANYON SAN BERNARDINO.CALIF.1-1-46.HER HUSBAND
ARTHUR R.EGGERS AGE 55 A SHERIFFS OFFICE CLERK LIVING IN THEIR
HOME AT 202 NO ROSEMEAD BLVD.TEMPLE CITY CALIF.WAS ARRESTED FOR
THE CRIME.1-22-46.(MOTIVE)REVENGE FOR MRS EGGERS ASSERTED DALLIA-
NCE WITH OTHER MEN. *SENTENCED TO DEATH S.Q. GAS CHAMBER. 7-16-46.*

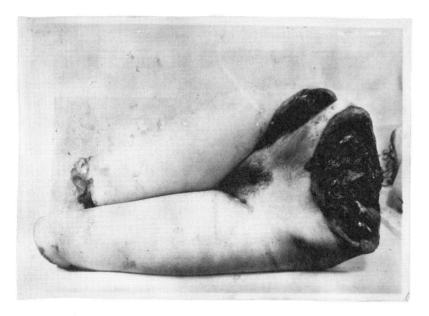

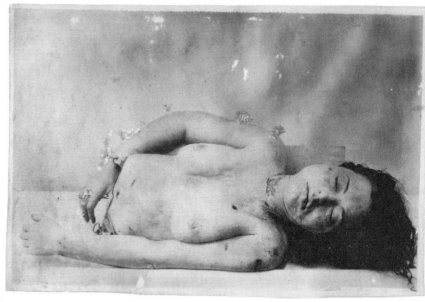

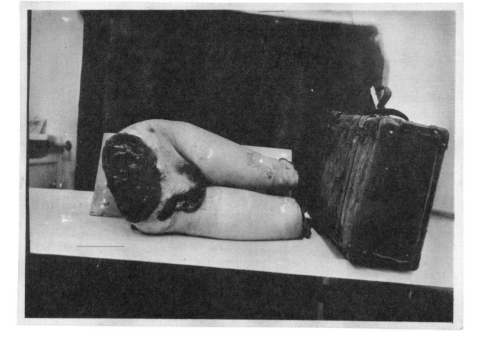

MISS SAMUELSON

KILLED BY RUTH
JUDD "ARIZONA
TIGER WOMAN"
CONVICTED OF
SLAYING TWO
WOMEN SHIPPED
THEM TO L.A. IN
A TRUNK. 1931

10-17-31.
CONFINED TO.
STATE HOSPITAL
PHOENIX ARIZONA.
"LIFE"

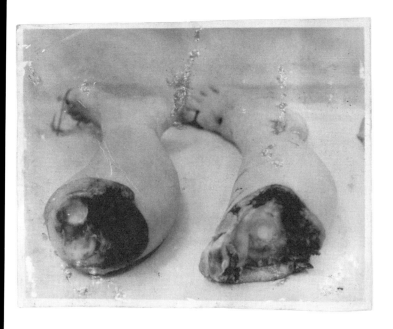

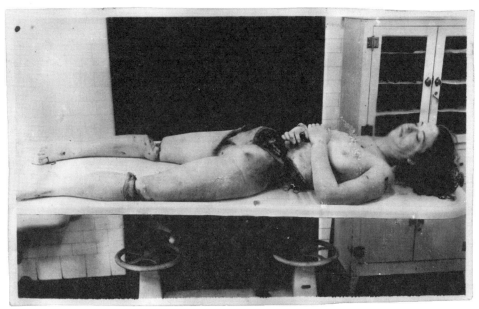

MISS SAMUELSON.

PHOTO'S
L.A. COUNTY MORGUE.

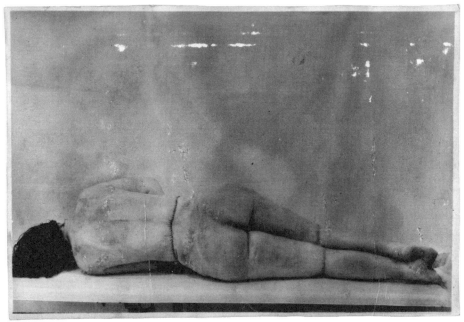

Fay Sudow A Prostitute and Fense
for Hot Jewelry,killed by a narcotic gang in Edendale eucalyptus
grove.In a suitcase found near the
body was Ioo strings of pearls 50
breastpins with diamonds 75 bracelets
December I2 I920. *UNSOLVED.*

L,A,First Blue-Beard Murder Case.
James P Watson,Age 42yrs,Married
twenty five wives,and Killed
Sixteene,of them,He would take
their money,jewelry,and bonds,
Watson would dig a grave,put Acid
on the body before he buried them.
He was sentenced to Life in S,Q,
5-18-20,He died in S,Q,hospital,
10-16-39.He was a Hermaphrodite.

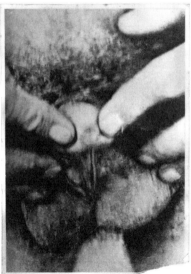

Blue-Beard Watson Organs a,
Hermaphrodite.

HE MARRIED 25 WIVES, KILLED ~~ELEVEN~~ 16 WIVES   USED ACID THEN BURIED THEM
5-18-20
(DIED IN SAN QUENTIN HOSPITAL 10-16-39)

TAKEN FROM
HIS WIVES
BY WATSON

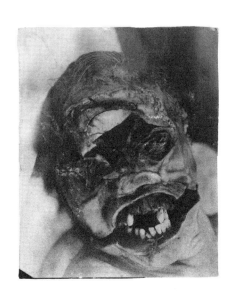

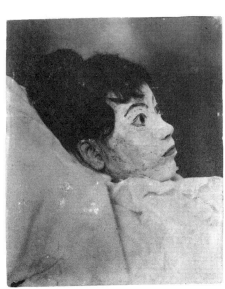

① NINA LEE DELONEY
THE LAST OF THE WIVES

②

③ SAME BODY

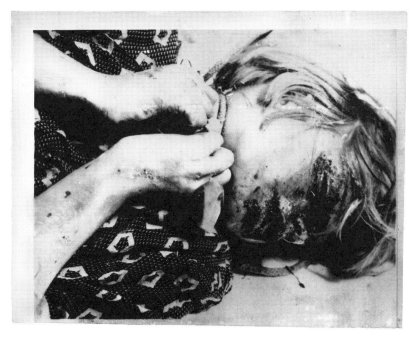

MELBA EVERETT
KILLED
BY, ALBERT DYER
INGLEWOOD CAL.
6-29-37.
"HANGED"
SAN QUENTIN
1938 9, YRS.

ALBERT. DYER.

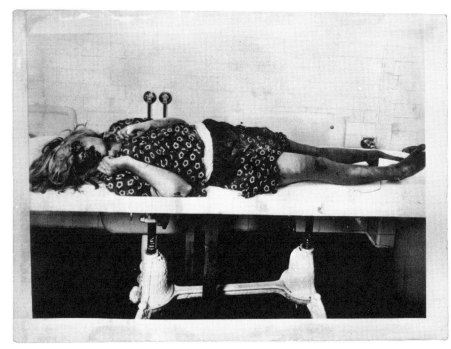

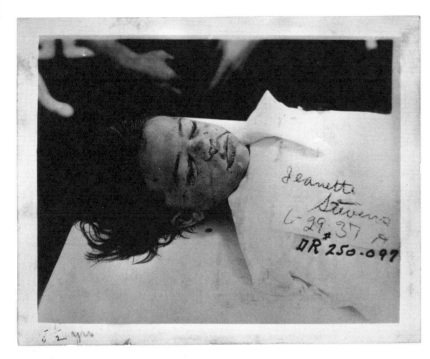

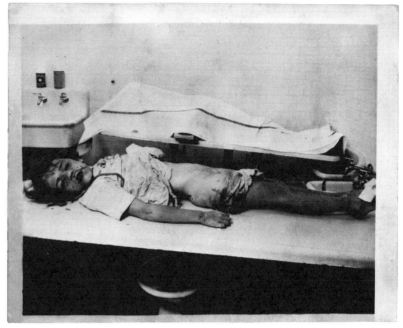

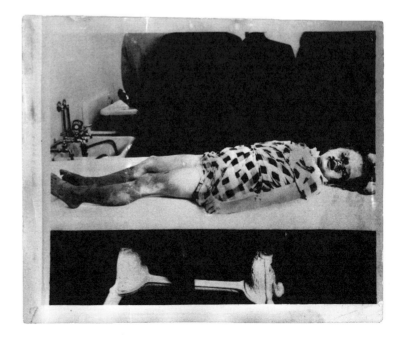

JEANETTE
STEVENS
KILLED BY
"ALBERT DYER"
INGLEWOOD CAL
6-29-37.
8½ YRS

MADELINE EVERETT KILLED BY
ALBERT DYER INGLEWOOD CAL 7 YRS

MRS DIANE SPARKS AGE 31 WIFE OF GEORGE E,SPARKS A LOS ANGELES POLICEMAN.HER
NUDE BODY WAS FOUND IN A SHALLOW PARTLY COVERED GRAVE IN LANAR CANYON.NEAR
ROSCOE CALIF.3-10-46.THEY LIVED AT 10822 CHANDLER BLVD NO HOLLYWOOD.RAMON GONZ-
ALES A NEIGHBOUR OF 5242 HARMONY AVE WAS HELD ON SUSPICION OF MURDERING HER AFTER
HIS GUN WAS FOUND NEAR THE BODY.HE WAS *FOUND NOT GUILTY 7-28-46.*

MRS. DIANE SPARKS
'Murder at the Vanities' Film Dancer Is Victim of
Real-Life Murder

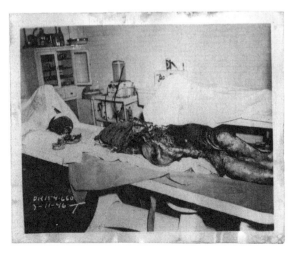 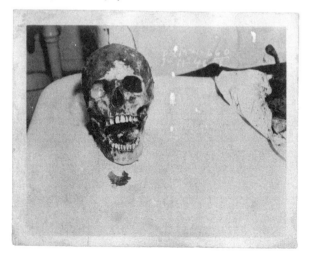

THE RED LIPSTICK MURDER.

MRS JEANNE AXFORD FRENCH AGE 40.(NURSE)
OF 3535MILITARY AVE,SAWTELL L.A.KILLED BY
                    ??.HER BODY WAS FOUND
IN A FIELD NEAR GRAND VIEW AVE,& NATIONAL
BLVD.L.A.2-10-47.SHE WAS STOMPED TO DEATH
BY A FIEND WHO CRUDELY PRINTED AN OBSCENE
PHRASE (FUCK YOU) ON HER CHEST.

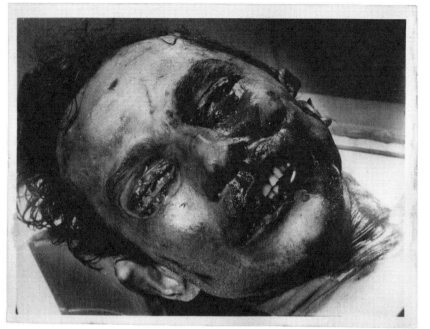
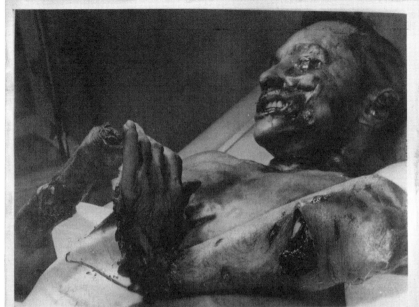
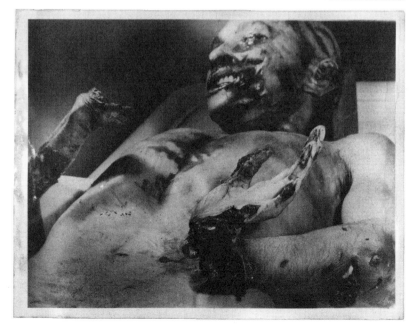

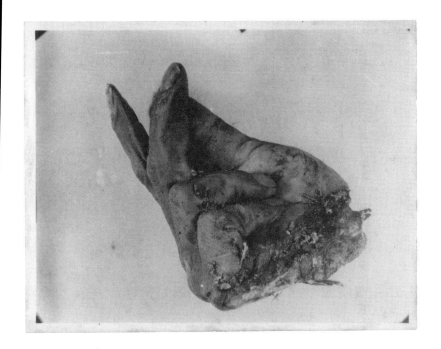

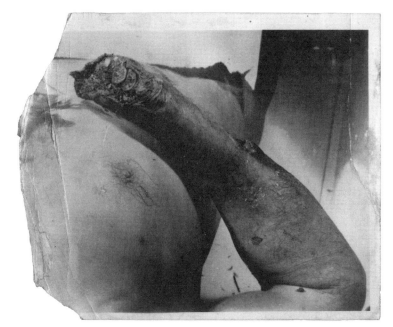

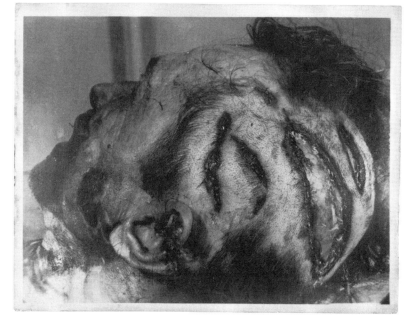

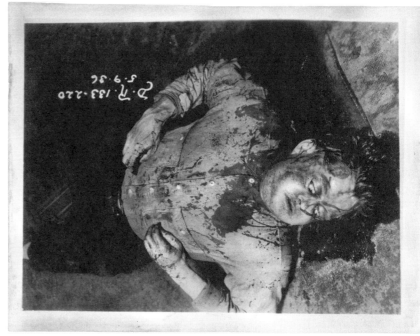

Murder in a Hobo camp unsolved L,A.Cal,5/9/36.

KILLED BY-?
IN A HOBO CAMP

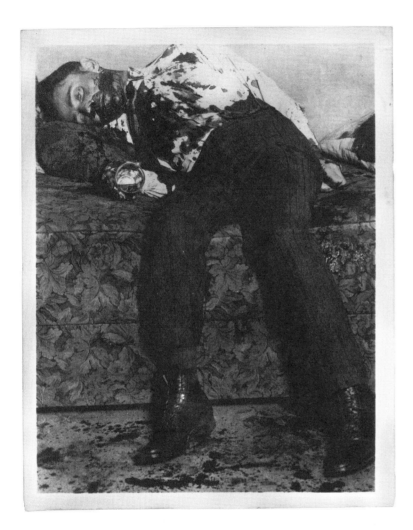

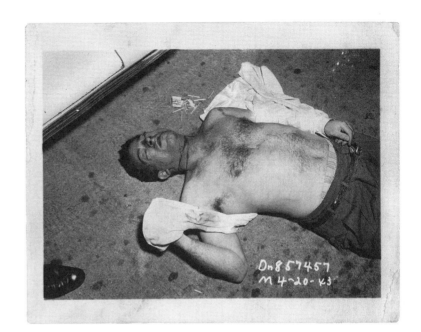

HARRY i KATZ MURDERED
11-10-24.

MURDER.

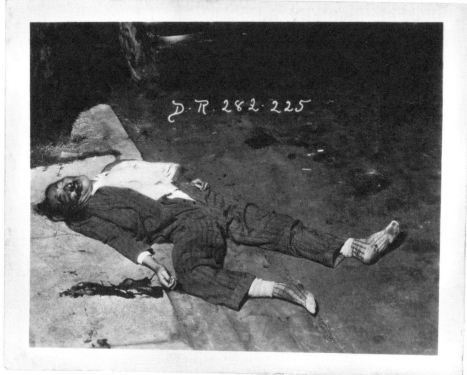

JAP KILLED BY NEGRO, HE TOOK 30¢ AND
HIS, WATCH. ARRESTED IN PALM SPRINGS.
2 TO 10 S.Q. L.A. CAL.

WALDMAR KLITZKE KILLED BY
OWNER OF A HOT DOG STAND, OVER PAYMENT
OF A 10¢ HOT DOG PICO AND OAK, ST L.A.

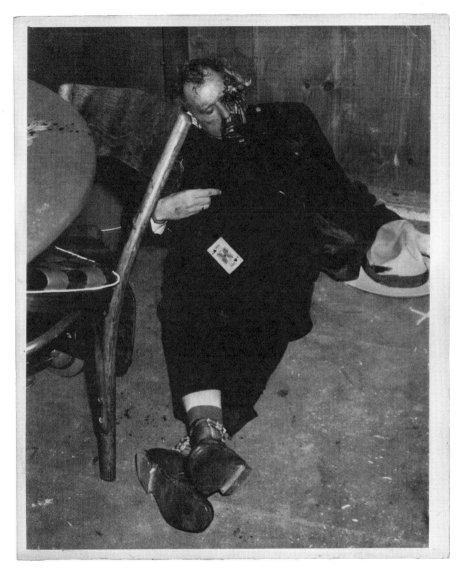

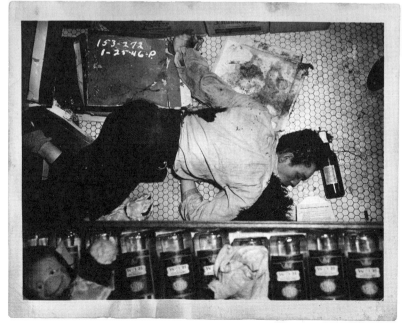

KING OF SPADE. MURDER.   3-8-42.
OFFICER L.N. BUNCH. L.A. POLICE. KILLED IN TWIN PALMS CAFE.
1819 REDONDO BEACH BLVD. GARDENA. 3-8-42, LYLE GILBERT AND.
JACK LOVELACE. SENTENCED TO LIFE. MAX GILBERT SENTENCED
TO LIFE. 8-5-42. ORVILLE HORGAN KILLED BY BUNCH.

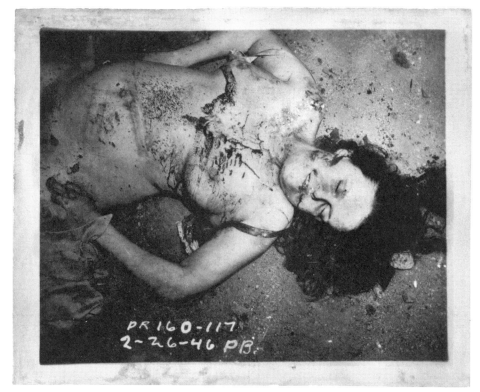

MISS MAY (CHUCKIE) DASPARRO AGE 32 A
PROSTITUTE. KILLED BY LEROY HARRIS
GEIGER AGE 24 IN A PARKING LOT AT
SIXTH & MAPLE ST OFF OF SKID ROW L.A.
CALIF. 2-26-46. HE HIT HER, STUFFED HIS
HANDKERCHIEF INTO HER MOUTH IN AN
ATTEMPT TO STILL HER WIERD CRIES. THEN
RIPPED HER CLOTHES OFF AND STABBED HER
22 TIMES WITH A KNIFE. HE WAS ARRESTED
AND 5 TO LIFE. 5-13-46 S.Q

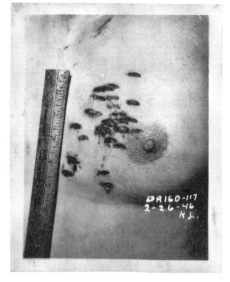

MISS LOUISE TEUBER
AGE 17 KILLED BY SEX FIEND
SAN DIEGO, CAL. 1936. "UNSOLVED"

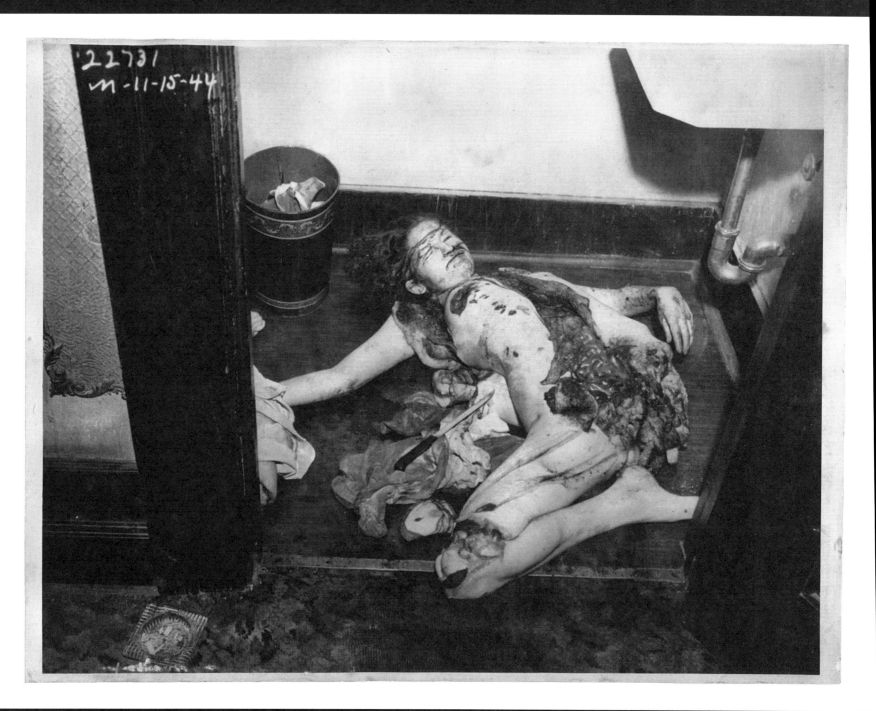

STEVE THE KILLER.
A
JACK THE RIPPER.

Otto Steven Wilson age 31, ship-
yard cook.met Mrs Virginia Lee
Griffin who lived at 1934 East
17th St L.A.Calif in a Skid Row
Beer Parlor at 326 So Hill St.
They went to a Hotel at 4th &
Main St with the idea of Prosti-
tution.He hit her stabbed her &
Cut her up.Photo of Mrs Griffin
age 25,on the Left.
Using the same Idea he took Mrs
Lillian Johnson age 38 of Compton
Calif,to a Hotel at 340 So Hill
St.He choked her to death &
carved her up with a razor blade.
Wilson was arrested by Patrolman
Harold E,Donlan in a Beer Parlor
on So Hill St,only a few doors
from the Hotel where Wilsons
second victim was found.
When arrested he was trying to
date up another women.
  L,A,Calif.11/15/44.
SENTENCED TO DEATH IN THE SAN
QUENTIN GAS CHAMBER. 7-5-45
DIED 9-20-46

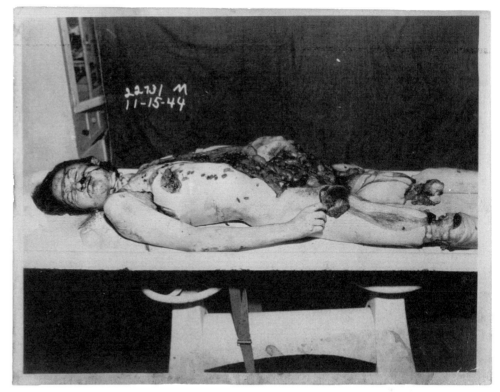

OTTO STEVEN WILSON.

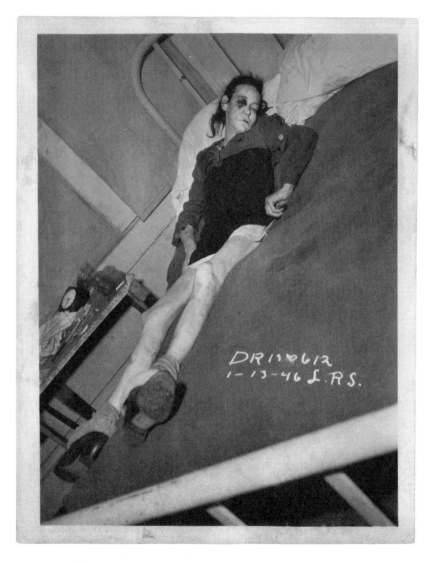

PAULA(SLIM)ANDERSON A PROSTITUTE
WITH 27 PRIORS KILLED BY   ?
AT 447 EAST 6TH ST L.A.CALIF.I-I3-46.

Miss Vivian Riley age 28 killed by
Vernon Spangler age 28 in his room at
705 West 6th St L.A.Cal.3/I7/45.He took
her body to the rear of a laundry at 703
West 6th St.2nd degree 5Yrs to Life,S.Q.

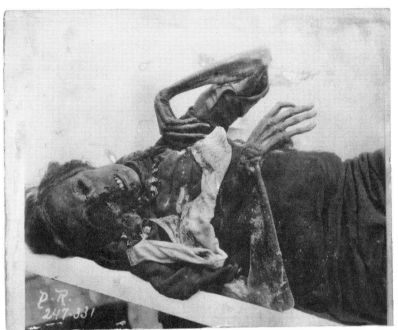
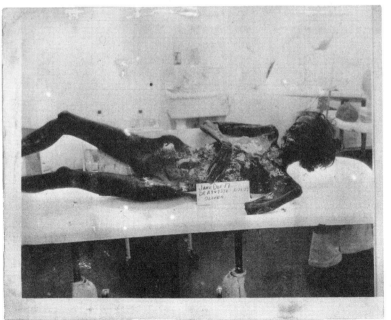

MRS ALICE JONES "STARVATION" 1937
(FOUND UNDER HER HOUSE)

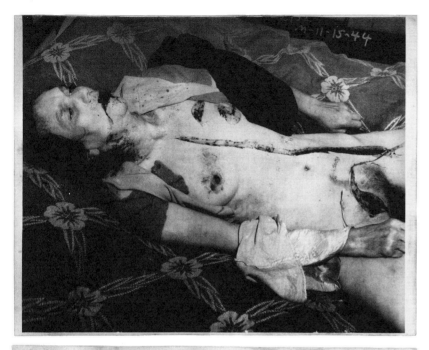

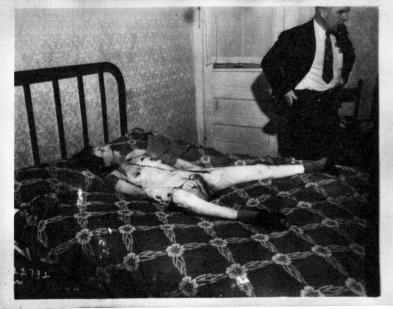

MURDER.-?

MURDER RAPE.AND ROBBERY.
MRS LILLIAN W STRATTON AGE 74 YRS.KILLED BY   ? ON THE LAWN OF HER HOME AT
479 PARK FRONT,SOUTH PARK,LA.9 20 42.MR STRATTON AGE 81 YRS WITH TEAR DIMMED EYES IS ON
THE RIGHT WITH A NEIGHBOUR.THE SHOCK DEFEATED HIS WILL TO LIVE,HE JOINED HIS WIFE IN
DEATH WITH A BROKEN HEART I 15 43.

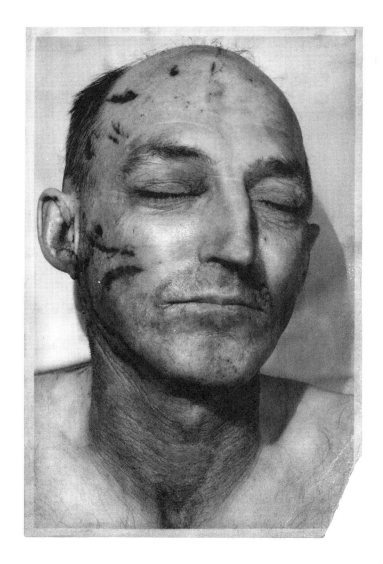 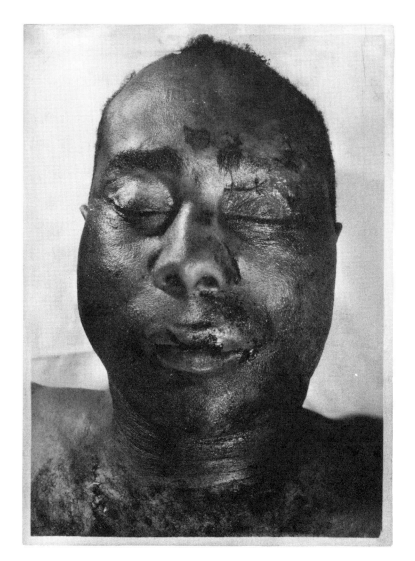

AUTO ACCIDENT

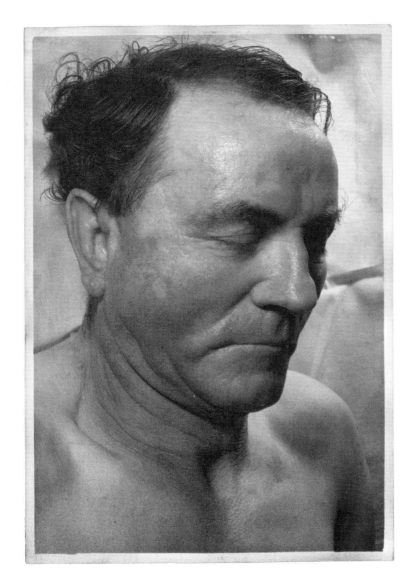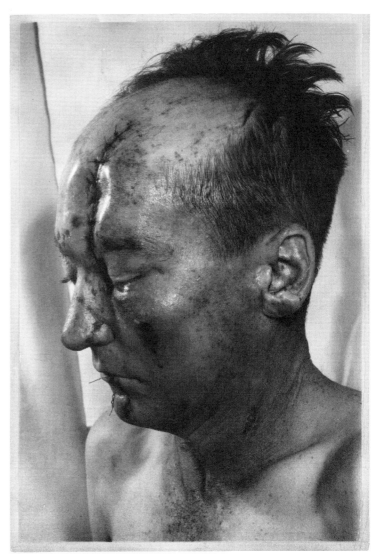

AUTO ACCIDENT

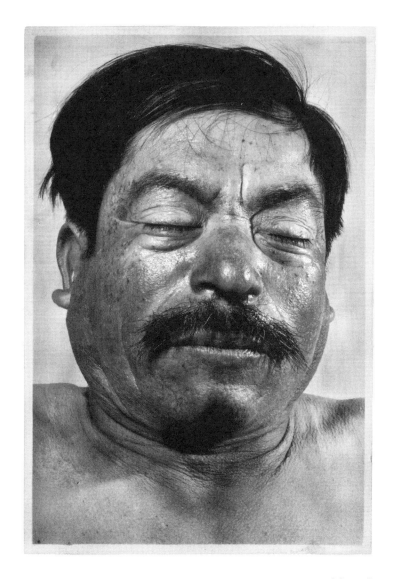 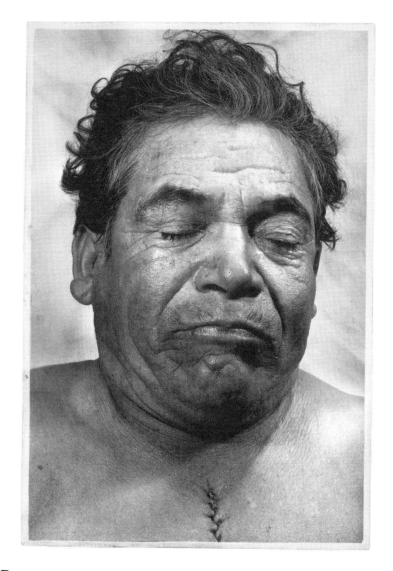

AUTO ACCIDENTS COUNTY MORGUE
SACRAMENTO .CAL.

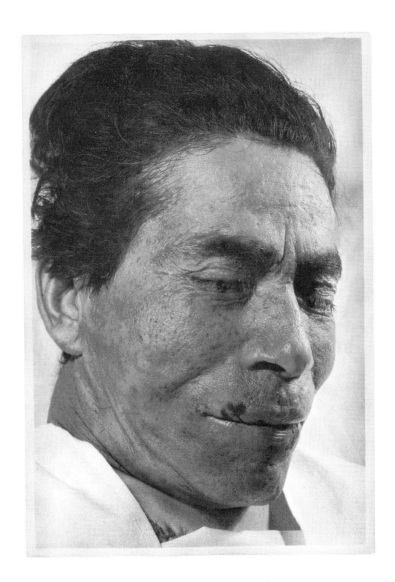

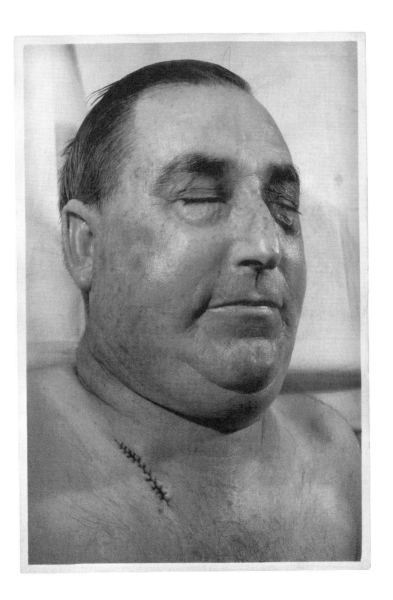

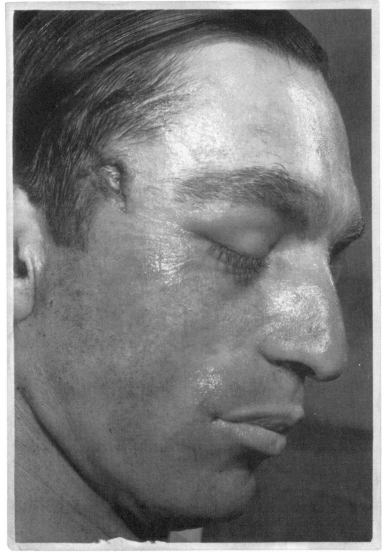

MURDER

VENTURO LEMOS KILLED BY ANTONIO GARCIA
7-21-33 "KNIFE"

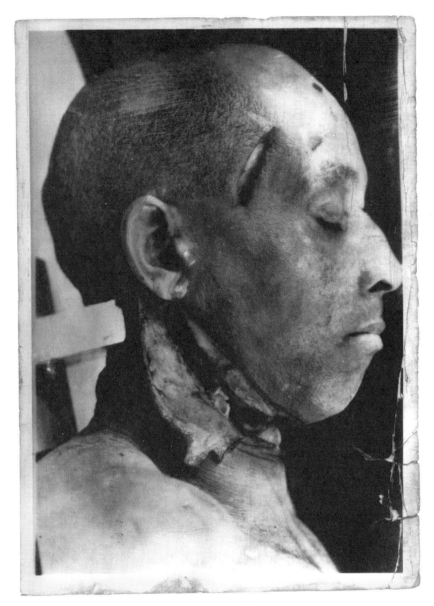

MURDER

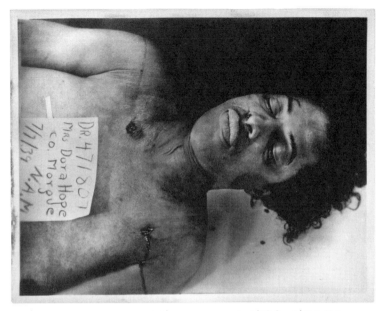

DORA HOPE KILLED BY HER HUSBAND
7-7-39.

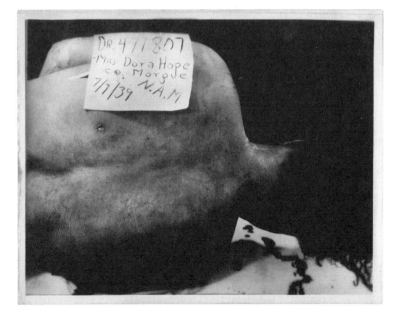

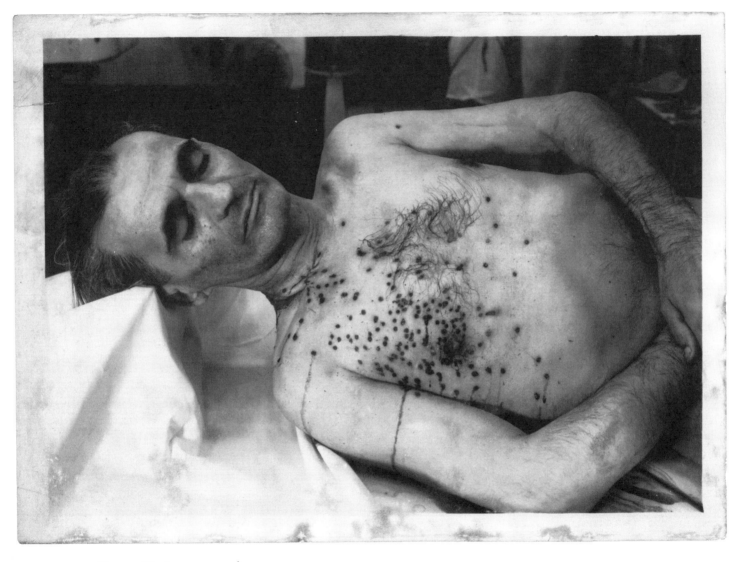

JACK. J. GLANUZINA SHOT BY HIS FORMER BARTENDER
EMMETT LEE FINCH AT 100 SO, GRAND AVE L.A.
7-30-42.   10-29-42. LIFE IN S.Q.

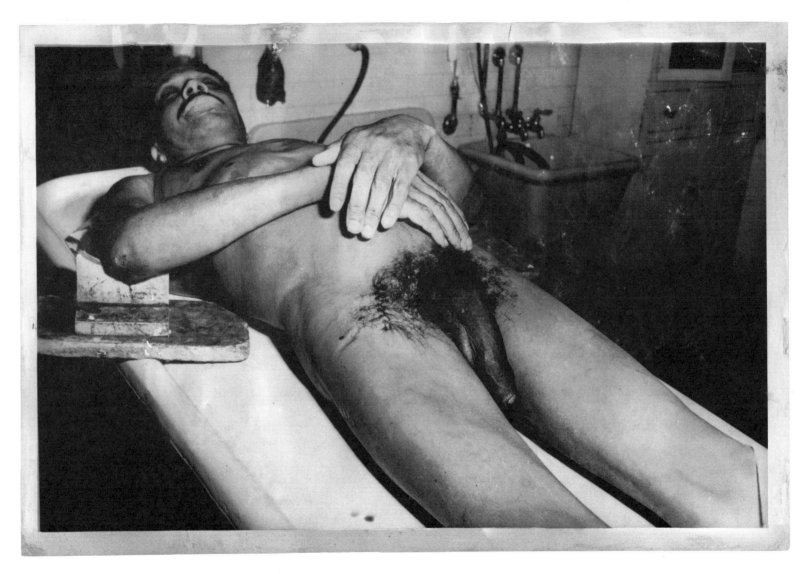

THE KING OF CENTRAL AVE MURDER.

JAMES ROGER SMITH NEGRO AGE 36.KILLED BY BENJAIME F TAYLOR
AGE 38.NEGRO.AT 236 EAST 2ND ST L.A.CAL.MAY 29TH 1945.10 PM.
MOTIVE JEALOUSLY OVER A NEGRO WOMAN.

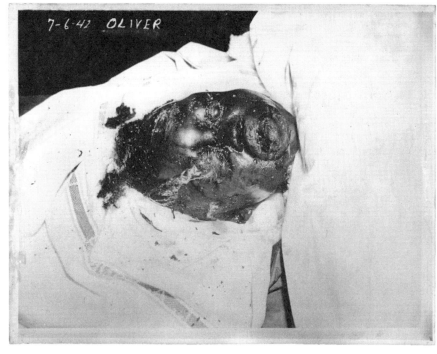

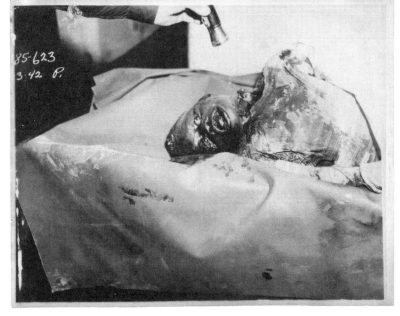

OSCAR "SNOOKY" RANKIN NEGRO,
7YRS KILLED BY EDWARD
GAINOUS 38YRS. NEGRO.
"STRANGLED" 7-6-42.
AFTER TWO TRIALS
HE WAS CONVICTED,
SENTENCED TO DEATH
S.Q 12-20-42.

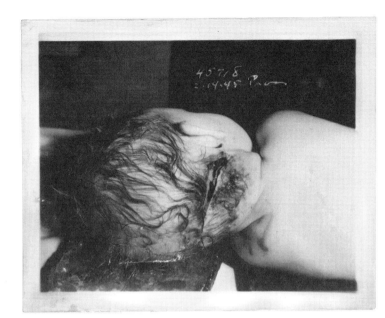

Marguerite Derdenger age 2I months killed
by the family pet Dog Woof.(Motive Jealously),I742 West Sixth St.L.A.Cal,2/I4/45.

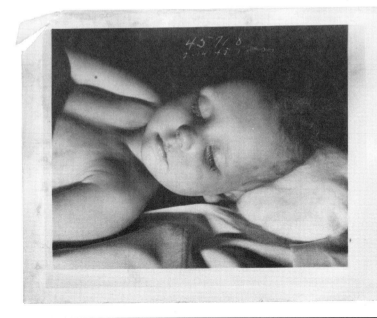

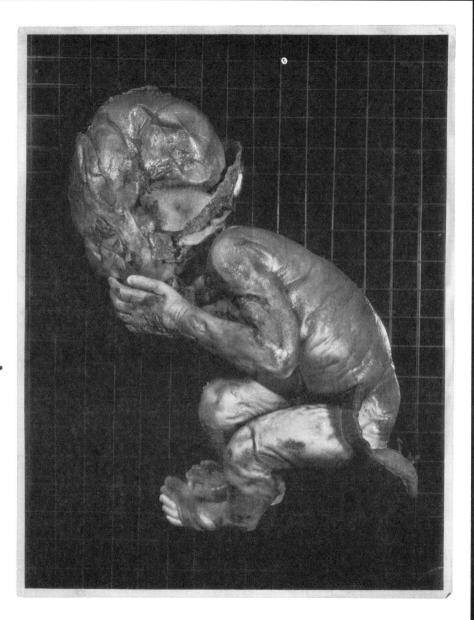

ABORTION CRIMINAL.
Found in P,E,Depot,L,A,Cal.I943.

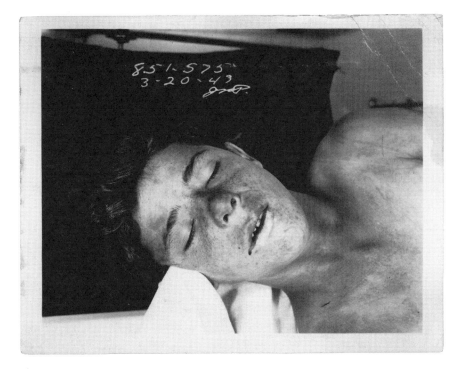

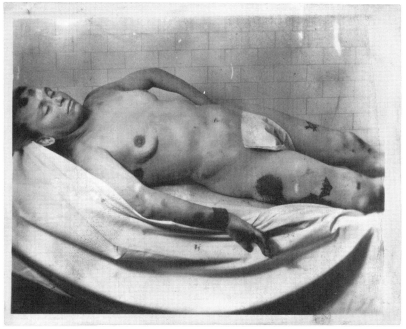

EUGENE UNDERWOOD AGE 14 YRS,ACCIDENTAL
HOMICIDE.HE WAS LEARNING JU-JUTSU AND
STRANGLED HIS SELF WHILE PRACTISING,HE
HAD CALLOUS MARKS ON HIS THROAT.L.A.CAL.

SUICIDE

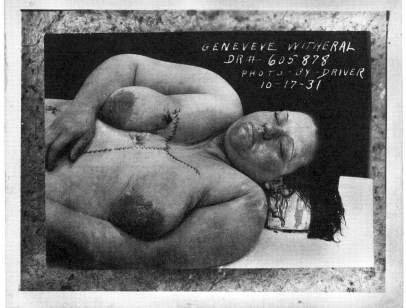

Accidental Homicide Monox Gas,L,A,Calif.

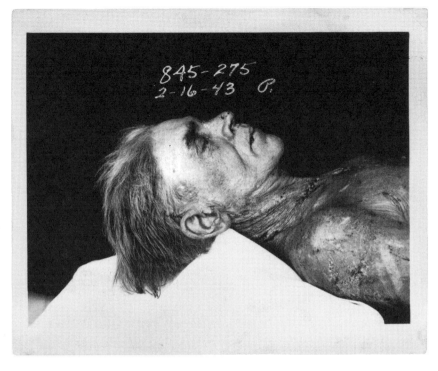

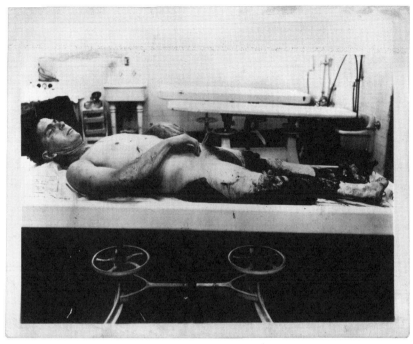

L.A.POLICE BRUTALITY.
J.L.WESTHOUSE ARRESTED FOR DRUNK DIED IN
CITY JAIL.HIS RELATION CLAIM HE WAS BEAT
UP IN JAIL.THE ABOVE PHOTO AND AUTOPSY
SHOWS HE DIED FROM FILTH,HE HAD WINE
SORES,SCALES,AND LICE IN HIS HAIR.

HIT BY A TRAIN.

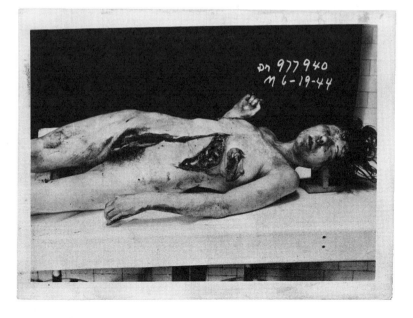

MARIE CASTANEDA AGE 29 KILLED BY HER
BOY FRIEND VERNON ARENSON.HE BROKE A
WINE BOTTLE AND CUT HER.6/19/44.L.A.Cal.
612½ No SPRING ST. LIFE IN S.Q. 7-4-44.

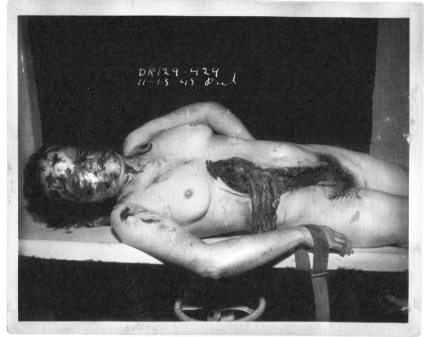

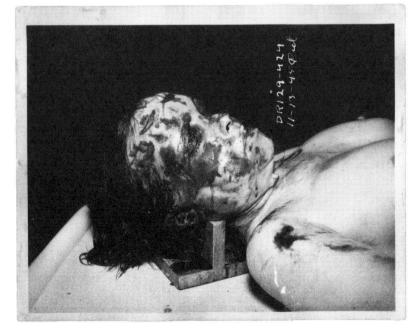

Mrs Florence Honeycutt age 38.Killed by her
husband John T Honeycutt age 32.He ripped
her to pieces with a carving knife while she
still was alive,then beat her with a meat
grinder.while her elderly mother looked on
horrified II-13-45. Roscoe.Calif.Honeycutt
an Ex-convict was found guilty of first degree
murder and sentenced to death in the S.Q.Lethal
Gas Chamber.2-I4-46. EXECUTED 2-7-47. S.Q.

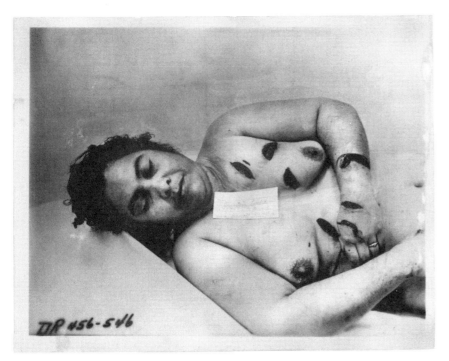

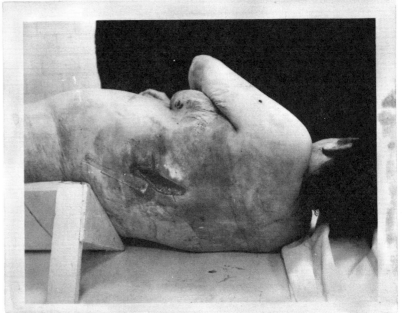

BENANCIA SALIDRA.
KILLED BY HER
SWEETHEART
"STAB" 5-16-39.
"JOSE GOMEZ." "LIFE"
MARIJUANA

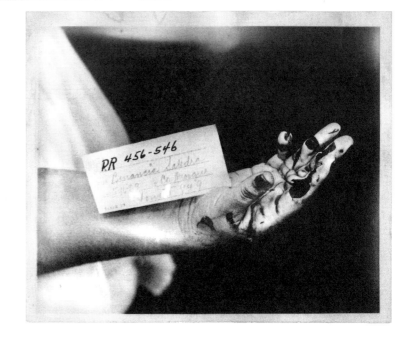

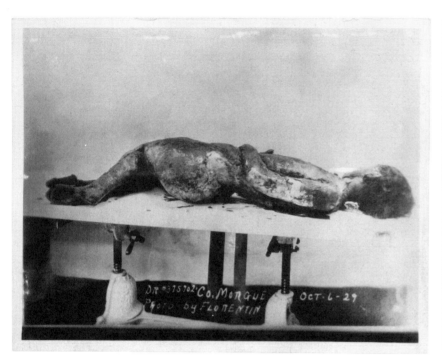 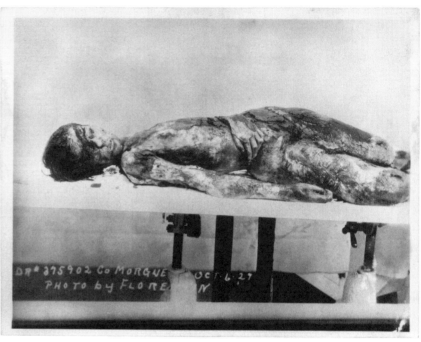

AN ATTEMPT RESURRECTION BY A CULT. VENICE CAL.
(MISS WILLA RHOADS. AGE 16 YRS.)

Minnie Sieber killed by her husband with an iron bar,512 E ave 28 L,A.
2-7-26.Chas Sieber was hanged in S,Q.

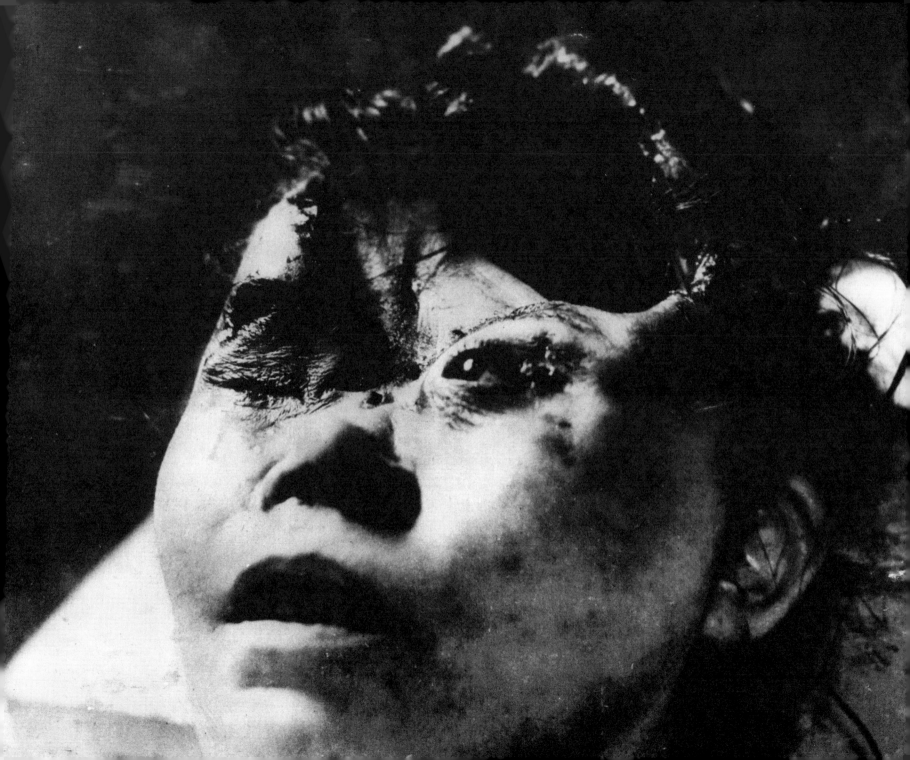

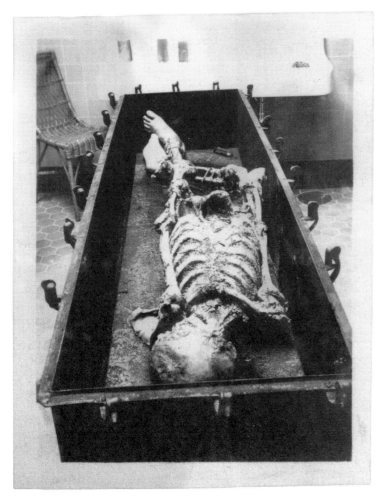

SUICIDE OAKLAND CAL.

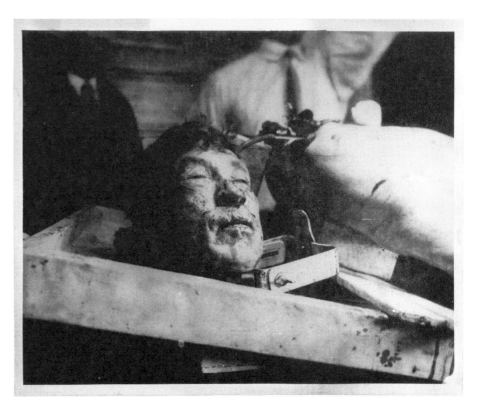

Jose Rodriquez killed by Tony Santeg,
He decapitated the head and put it in
a barrel of quick-lime,Hanged in S,Q.

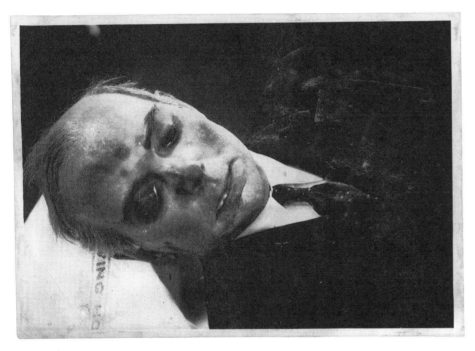

AFTER THREE MONTHS.

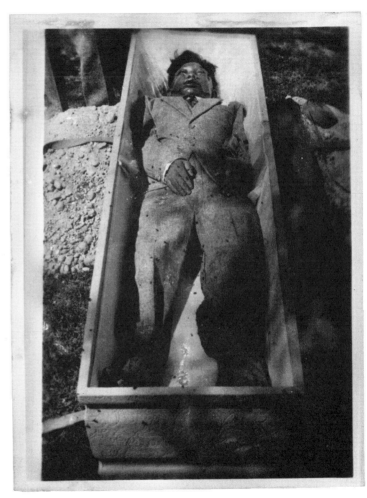

LOUIE FOOK SUICIDE
SAN ANTONIO TEXAS.
"EXHUMED"
SLAYER OF LOUIE GAR. CHUN
IN L.A. CAL.

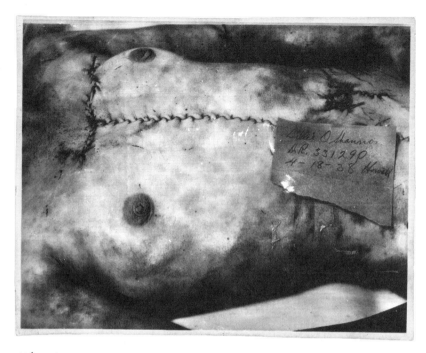

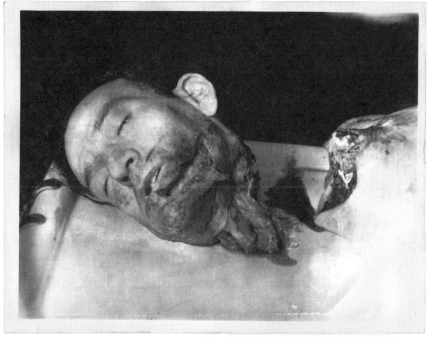

BILLIE O SHANNON KILLED BY MARIE
WOODS. OVER A MARIJUANA. CIGARETTE

MURDER "AXE" DECAPITATE

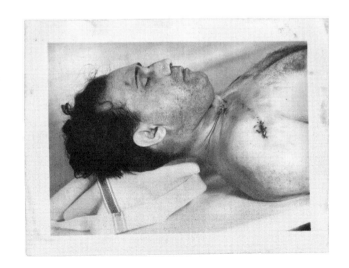

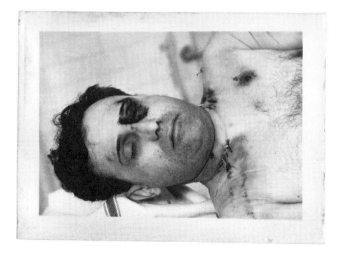

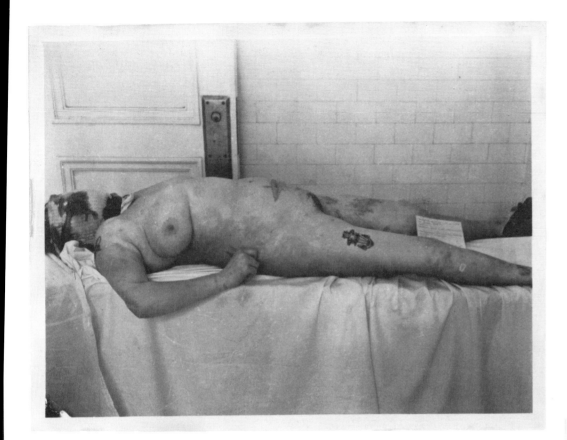

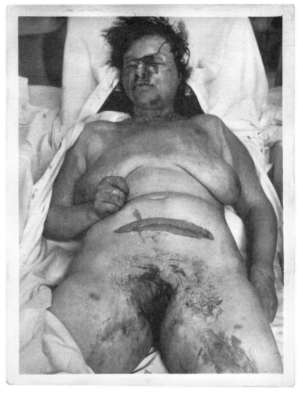

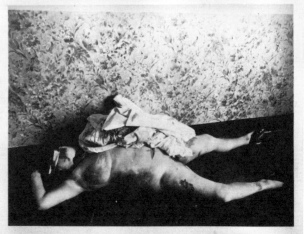

MRS IRENE McCARTHY KILLED BY W<u>M</u> JOHANSEN.
12-40 SAN FRANCISCO. CAL. HE WAS EXECUTED
IN; SAN QUENTIN. LETHAL GAS CHAMBER. 9-6-41-
"HE KILLED THREE WOMEN"

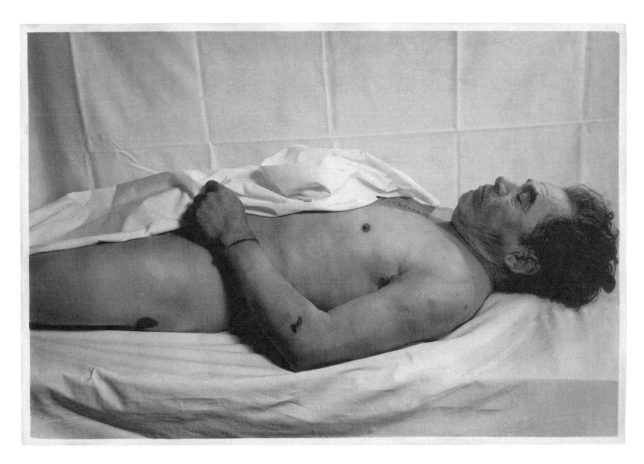

SUICIDE

HUMAN SKIN COMPLETE FOUND IN THE CITY DUMP
12/30/32. UNSOLVED. L.A. CAL.

NEVADA STATE PEN.
CARSON CITY, NEVADA.

GAS CHAMBER CARSON CITY NEVADA.

SING SING PRISON
ELECT CHAIR. 1928.

LETHAL GAS CHAMBER SAN QUENTIN.

LEAVENWORTH FED PEN KANSAS.

SAN QUENTIN PEN.
THE LARGEST PEN IN U.S.A.

SAN QUENTIN, THANKSGIVING DAY 1936

MESS HALL, SAN QUENTIN. 1941.

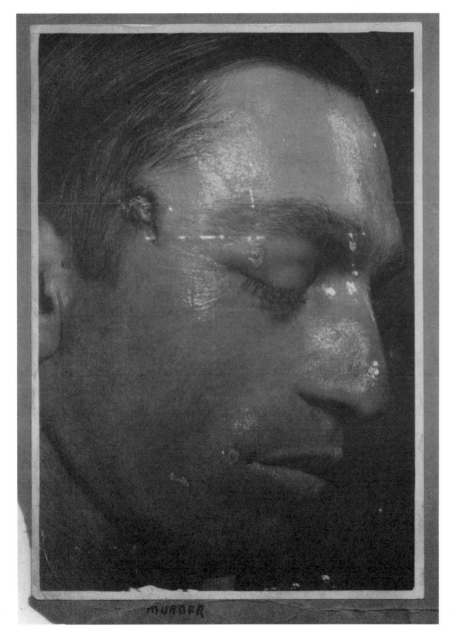

BEFORE

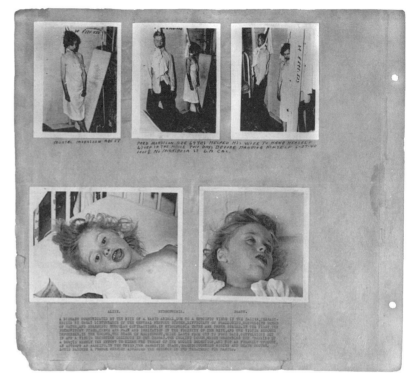

Most of the photographs in this book were retouched, using Adobe Photoshop™ 3.03 on a Power Macintosh 7100/80. Once the half-century old scrapbook was scanned, the individual photographs were straightened, isolated, and the paper behind them digitally removed. Scratches, flaking, and other marks that obscured the photographs were nearly always retouched. We took pains to retain the integrity of the photograph; all retouching remained cosmetic. Photos were left unaltered where it would have meant recreating a critical portion of the image. The photos were not retouched to perfection, only to enhance clarity.

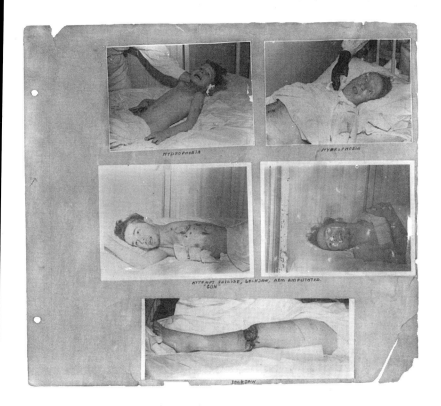

Black and white tonal levels were also adjusted, to bring out details in shadows, maintain subtle shading in lighter areas, and compensate as much as possible for subtle changes during printing. Certain photographs in the scrapbook were originally positioned sideways or upside down, and their placement has been preserved.

The book in your hands remains as faithful as possible to the look and feel of Huddleston's book as he first assembled it over fifty years ago.

— Sean Tejaratchi

Editor

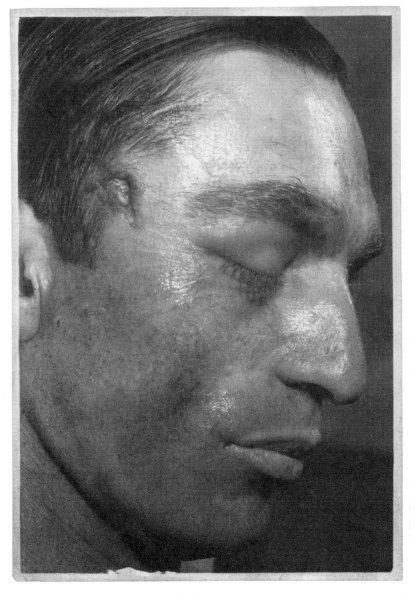

MURDER

AFTER

also available from Feral House

Muerte! Death in Mexican Popular Culture *Edited by Harvey Stafford*

Mexico is a country obsessed with blood and gore. The biggest selling magazines, *Alarma!* and *Peligro!*, week after week promote the most extreme examples of death they can find. Why does Mexican culture, a strange amalgam of Catholicism and Santeria, go so far with bloody sensationalism?

The photographs within Muerte! were largely snapped by the biggest photographers from Mexican tabloids, and are printed in this book for the first time. *Muerte!* also includes text from Diego Rivera, Eduardo Matos Moctezuma, Jorge Alberto Manrique, Alberto Hijar and Victor Fosada explaining Mexican death-consciousness.

Editor Harvey Stafford's own stunning paintings, inspired by Mexican tabloid photography, are also included, along with Stafford's saga about confronting Mexico's tabloids in person.

10 × 8 ◆ 102 pgs ◆ full color ◆ ISBN 0-922915-59-8 ◆ $16.95

Lords of Chaos The Bloody Rise of the Satanic Metal Underground
Michael Moynihan and Didrik Søderlind

Michael Moynihan and Didrik Søderlind uncover black metal's grim legacy of suicide, murder and terrorism. This incredible book features hundreds of rare photos and exclusive interrogations with leaders of demonic bands who believe the greater evil spawns the greatest glory.

"The integration of storytelling and in-depth interviews, as well as bringing to light a certain philosophy on a rather blood-stained reality, thrusts this beyond anything previously written about the 'black metal scene.' . . . a book worth reading by people within the scene to get and 'outside gaze' at themselves."—Maniac, singer of *Mayhem*

6 × 9 ◆ 358 pgs ◆ photos ◆ ISBN 0-922915-48-2 ◆ $16.95

Apocalypse Culture II *Edited by Adam Parfrey*

We've been told that the original *Apocalypse Culture* ruined marriages, created fistfights, and inspired people for life. Reviewers claimed *Apocalypse Culture* was "the new book of revelation" and "the terminal documents of our time." *Apocalypse Culture II* breaks the editor's arrogant promise that no sequel edition would ever appear. Herein find over 62 new articles and 200 photos and illustrations delineating the Forbidden Zone, the psychic maelstrom that everyone knows exists but fearfully avoids.

"Adam Parfrey's astonishing, un-put-downable and absolutely brilliant compilation, *Apocalypse Culture II*, will blow a hole through your mind the size of JonBenét's fist."—Jerry Stahl, author of *Permanent Midnight* and *Perv—a Love Story*

6 × 9 ◆ 470 pgs ◆ full color section ◆ ISBN 0-922915-57-1 ◆ $18.95

To order from Feral House:

Domestic orders add $4 shipping for first item, $1.50 each additional item. Amex, MasterCard, Visa, checks and money orders are accepted. (CA state residents add 8% tax.)
Canadian orders add $7 shipping for first item, $2 each additional item. Other countries add $11 shipping for first item, $9 each additional item.
Non-U.S. originated orders must be international money order or check drawn on a U.S. bank only.

Send orders to: Feral House, P.O. Box 13067, Los Angeles, CA 90013

www.feralhouse.com